STAFFORD LIBRARY
COLUMBIA COLLEGE
COLUMBIA, MO 65216

 Climate and Literature

 # Climate and Literature

Reflections of Environment

Edited by Janet Pérez
and Wendell Aycock

Texas Tech University Press

STUDIES IN COMPARATIVE LITERATURE
NUMBER 25

©Copyright 1995 Texas Tech University Press

All rights reserved. No portion of this book may be reproduced in any form or by any means, including electronic storage and retrieval systems, except by explicit, prior written permission of the publisher except for brief passages excerpted for review and critical purposes.

This book was set in 10 on 12 Garamond and printed on acid-free paper that meets the guidelines for permanence and durability of the Committee on Production Guidelines for Book Longevity of the Council on Library Resources. ∞

Printed in the United States of America

Library of Congress Catagloging-in-Publication Data
Climate and literature : reflections of environment / edited by Janet Pérez and Wendell Aycock.
    p. cm. — (Studies in comparative literature, ISSN 0899-2193 ; no. 25)
    Contents: Writing the bodies of water : the clash of the lasting and the catastrophic in the Odes of Horace / Rosemary M. Nielsen and Robert H. Solomon — Climate as science and metaphor in the writings of Jehuda Halevi / Stephen T. Newmyer — Astral and tidal phenomena, earthquake prediction, and The astronomical clock of Juan de Barrenechea / Robert J. Morris — Zola's uses of climate in The land / Wendell McClendon — The role of climate in twentieth-century Spanish American fiction / George R. McMurray — The endless rains of death and desolation in García Márquez's short stories / Clementina R. Adams — Creating an atmosphere : depiction of climate in the works of Gabriel García Márquez / Gary S. Elbow — The weather as a story element in four short works from Latin America / Paul Nelson — Heat, water, and stars in Pedro Páramo / Cida Chase — Ices everlasting and passions perverted : the physical and moral climate of Puig's anti-utopia / Leonard A. Cheever — Influence of climate on the cultures of the jungle as perceived by two Latin American novelists / Raquel Romeu — Climate and identity in the literature of the French Antilles / Jack Jordan — Afro-Cuban culture, ecology, and climate in La comparsa by Felipe Pichardo Moya / Luis A. Jiménez.
    ISBN 0-89672-354-2
    1. Climate in literature. 2. Weather in literature. 3. Setting (Literature) I. Pérez, Janet. II. Aycock. Wendell M. III. Series: Studies in comparative literature (Lubbock, Tex.) ; no. 25.
PN56.C612C55 1995
809'.9336—dc20   95-36736
                                                                                         CIP

95 96 97 98 99 00 01 02 03 / 9 8 7 6 5 4 3 2 1

Texas Tech University Press
P. O. Box 41037
Lubbock, Texas 79409-1037 USA
1-800-832-4042

In memory of
Wendell McClendon

STUDIES IN COMPARATIVE LITERATURE
TEXAS TECH UNIVERSITY PRESS

*James Joyce: His Place in World Literature
*From Surrealism to the Absurd
Franz Kafka: His Place in World Literature
Modern American Fiction: Insights and Foreign Lights
*William Faulkner: Prevailing Verities and World Literature
Joseph Conrad: Theory and World Fiction
Albert Camus' Literary Milieu: Arid Lands
Ethnic Literature since 1776: The Many Voices of America, Part One and Part Two
Ibero-American Letters in a Comparative Perspective
Classical Mythology in Twentieth-Century Thought and Literature
Shakespeare's Art from a Comparative Perspective
The Teller and the Tale: Aspects of the Short Story
Calderón de la Barca at the Tercentenary: Comparative Views
Johann Wolfgang von Goethe: One Hundred and Fifty Years of Continuing Vitality
Women World Walkers: New Dimensions of Science Fiction and Fantasy
Myths and Realities of Contemporary French Theater
War and Peace: Perspectives in the Nuclear Age
Film and Literature: A Comparative Approach to Adaptation
Literature and Anthropology
The Spanish Civil War in Literature
The Body and the Text: Comparative Essays in Literature and Medicine
The Literature of Emigration and Exile
Epic and Epoch
Climate and Literature

*Out of print

Preface

The purpose of Studies in Comparative Literature is to explore literatures of various cultures and linguistic groups in comparison with one another and to compare literature with other disciplines or fields of study. First published in 1968, volumes of the series have derived from annual comparative literature symposia founded by Wolodymyr T. Zyla under the auspices of the Interdepartmental Committee on Comparative Literature at Texas Tech. In subsequent years, the series flourished, and volumes have been devoted to the study of authors (e.g., Kafka, Camus, Shakespeare), genres (e.g., the short story, science fiction), and movements and themes (e.g., surrealism, mythology).

This volume focuses on climate and literature, or the study of how authors have illustrated the impact of weather and various other features of climate upon their characters, milieu, and themes. Although an all-inclusive study of the topic would stretch beyond the bounds of this small volume, herein are found representative chapters pertaining to the classic period, the renaissance period in France, and nineteenth- and twentieth-century literature from various countries. All of these chapters seek to illustrate how literary artists have made especial use of some feature of climate.

Wendell Aycock
Series Editor

Contents

Introduction	1
Writing the Bodies of Water: The Clash of the Lasting and the Catastrophic in the *Odes* of Horace *Rosemary M. Nielsen and Robert H. Solomon*	7
Climate as Science and Metaphor in the Writings of Jehuda Halevi *Stephen T. Newmyer*	19
Astral and Tidal Phenomena, Earthquake Prediction, and *The Astronomical Clock* of Juan de Barrenechea *Robert J. Morris*	29
Zola's Uses of Climate in *The Land* *Wendell McClendon*	43
The Role of Climate in Twentieth-Century Spanish American Fiction *George R. McMurray*	55
The Endless Rains of Death and Desolation in García Márquez's Short Stories *Clementina R. Adams*	65
Creating an Atmosphere: Depiction of Climate in the Works of Gabriel García Márquez *Gary S. Elbow*	73

The Weather as A Story Element in Four Short Works
    from Latin America   83
Paul Nelson

Heat, Water, and Stars in *Pedro Páramo*   89
Cida Chase

Ices Everlasting and Passions Perverted: The Physical
    and Moral Climate of Puig's Anti-Utopia   99
Leonard A. Cheever

Influence of Climate on the Cultures of the Jungle
    as Perceived by Two Latin American Novelists   107
Raquel Romeu

Climate and Identity in the Literature of the French Antilles   115
Jack Jordan

Afro-Cuban Culture, Ecology, and Climate in "La comparsa"
    by Felipe Pichardo Moya   123
Luis A. Jiménez

Notes on the Authors   131

 Introduction

Endangered species, acid rain, global warming and the ills of pollution, deforestation and desertification figure among almost daily reminders of the fragility of Earth's ecosystem, and climate plays a prominent role in many of these. On the threshold of a new milennium, the human race looks to the stars and contemplates the construction of micro-climates in space, yet has neither learned to conserve the resources of this small planet nor to control its climate. Drought and famine in Africa, catastrophic floods in China, India, Bangladesh, and along the Mississippi-Missouri River system in the American Midwest combine with the foreseeable devastation of annual typhoon and hurricane seasons, tornadoes and blizzards, among other egregious examples of climate's potential for havoc. Such exceptional episodes make the news while climate's more characteristic, benign moods are relegated to media oblivion.

History's protagonists have ignored climate at their peril: Hannibal found it more devastating than the legions of Rome. Both Napoleon and Hitler saw their hitherto irresistible armies defeated by the Russian winter, while a storm decimated Phillip II's "Invincible Armada." Climate's exceptional moments dwarf epic protagonists, as do its extremes, recorded in Jack London's tales of the Yukon and José Eustasio Rivera's anthropophagic drama of the all-devouring jungle in *La vorágine*, to mention only two examples. The challenges of deserts and polar regions offer ready-made literary situations, but such extreme climates constitute only a small portion of those portrayed in literature.

Such historic and literary commemorations of climate attest to the ubiquitous nature of a phenomenon whose extremes may vary but whose presence is inescapable and whose long-term changes, even if minimal, may have disastrous effects (cf. global warming, the "greenhouse effect," and the hole in the ozone). These considerations plus climate's power over humanity's food supply suffice to make it a universal concern. Humanity's collective experience, reflected in language, has resulted in numerous figurative and colloquial expressions involving weather and climate.

Ubiquitous and omnipresent, climate has transcended the domain of weather as a long-term phenomenon, becoming synonymous with environment and atmosphere. The essays to follow focus upon ancient and modern literary reflections of climates real and imagined. Reflections of contemporary concern for the environment and ecological problems, by no means exclusively the domain of modern literature or the industrialized nations, appear in varying degrees and forms in the national literatures represented in these essays. The studies, some comparative and others interdisciplinary, employ a variety of methodologies and critical approaches and include works drawn from Classical, English, French, and Latin American literatures.

Rosemary Nielsen and Robert Solomon examine the implications of poetic images of a world in elemental transition in Horace's "Parade Odes," discerning two contrasting treatments of the fluid world. In "Writing the Bodies of Water: The Clash of the Lasting and the Catastrophic in the *Odes* of Horace," Lucretius with his view of the "mortal" physical elements in *De Rerum Natura* provides the point of departure for the study of water-motifs and the interplay of philosophical and physical climates.

Centuries later, the medieval Jewish philosopher-physician-poet Jehuda Halevi of Toledo, a fervent precursor of Zionism, employed elements drawn from Jewish scientific and climatological thought in efforts to stimulate his readers' desire to return to the homeland. In "Climate as Science and Metaphor in the Writings of Jehuda Halevi," Stephen T. Newmyer contends that Halevi's scientific rhetoric, derived from Talmudic medical lore (and more remotely from classical Greek climatology) undergirds his argument that the peculiarly salutary climate of the Holy Land makes it most suitable for a restored Jewish homeland.

Robert J. Morris turns to the incipient Enlightenment in Spanish America and an obscure eighteenth-century academician in Lima for the basis of his study of early meteorological observation and forecasting in "Astral and Tidal Phenomena, Earthquake Prediction, and *The Astronomical Clock* of Juan de Barrenechea." As a colleague of Peralta de Barnuevo, an internationally-known astronomer, Barrenechea shared Peralta's special interest in studying the sun, moon and tides in their relation to earthquakes, and developed a chart for "perpetual prediction" of natural deaths, ebb tides and earthquakes.

In "Zola's Uses of Climate in *The Land*," Wendell McClendon demonstrates via a close reading of one of Zola's most naturalistic works that uses of climate, the principal element of realistic detail of the physical milieu, are more artistic than mimetic, and that the novelist's artistic rendering of reality both informs and affirms the naturalist's agenda and its outcomes. Zola is influenced by literary conventions, including images of climate and seasonal cycles, the connections between the seasons and four elements (earth, air, fire, water), and traditional or clichéd associations between the seasons and stages of human life, although he makes significant modifications.

George R. McMurray provides a preliminary overview of a vast and far-ranging topic in "The Role of Climate in Twentieth-Century Spanish American Fiction." Somewhat more detailed treatment is accorded the use of climate to foreshadow or reinforce mood in Martín Luis Guzmán's *La sombra del caudillo* (The Leader's Shadow), Elena Poniatowska's *Dear Diego*, and Antonio Skármeta's *Nothing Happened*. Carlos Fuentes's "Chac Mool," Jorge Luis Borges's "The Gospel According to Mark," Juan Rulfo's "We're Very Poor" and *Pedro Páramo*, José Donoso's "China" and "The Güero," and especially García Márquez's *One Hundred Years of Solitude* are analyzed in relation to the special prominence of rain. McMurray also studies the use of climate to create humor in works of García Márquez, Vargas Llosa, Isabel Allende and Carmen Naranjo, closing with a look at Octavio Paz's metaphorical *Tiempo nublado* (Cloudy Weather).

The focus of Clementina R. Adams in "The Endless Rains of Death and Desolation in García Márquez's Short Stories" is upon several pieces of brief fiction wherein the precipitation is prolonged intolerably or reaches unbearable extremes. Heat, humidity, and destructive floods also figure in this writer's stories foregrounding the special nature of rain in Aracataca, Barranquilla, and other towns of Colombia's Atlantic Coast.

Gary S. Elbow brings to bear the perspective of a geographer in "Creating an Atmosphere: Depiction of Weather in the Work of Gabriel García Márquez." Wind and aridity set the mood and subsequently determine the fate of Eréndira, whose life transpires in the arid coastal zone on the western side of the Guajira Peninsula, while *One Hundred Years of Solitude* and "Monologue of Isabel Watching it Rain in Macondo" are set on the Caribbean Coast at the foot of the precipitous Sierra Nevada de Santa Marta, an area averaging an annual rainfall of sixty-four inches. Elbow stresses that García Márquez writes of areas characterized by climatological anomalies.

Paul Nelson examines "The Weather as a Story Element in Four Short Works from Latin America," specifically in pieces of brief fiction by Colombians Hernando Téllez and García Márquez, contemporary Panamanian Enrique Jaramillo Leví, and the earlier post-naturalist Chilean, Baldomero Lillo. Viewing the literary manipulation of weather as a variant of the pathetic fallacy, Nelson specifies that it is not used sentimentally but to underscore the oppressive situations of characters. In Téllez's "Espuma y nada más" (Nothing but Foam), García Márquez's "Un día de éstos" (One of These Days), and Jaramillo Leví's "El cortejo" (The Funeral Procession), the central climatological motif is stifling, oppressive heat, while Lillo uses a contrasting climate, the cold, windy, rainy Chilean winter, to foreshadow the starvation of his protagonist, a striking miner, "frozen out" by the all-powerful mining company.

Cida Chase examines "Heat, Water and Stars in *Pedro Páramo*" as elements having power to illuminate some of the mysteries and uncertainties in Rulfo's masterpiece. Passages referring to climate lack the pervasive orality characterizing the remainder of the novel, becoming instead diaphanous, lyrical and suggestive. Rulfo's abundant climatological allusions function to present Comala as an unbearably hot place with rarified atmosphere, suffocating its residents. Rain and humidity in the novel are associated primarily with a happier past. Chase also briefly analyzes images of light and heavenly bodies.

Leonard A. Cheever's focus is upon the interconnectivity of physical climate and the metaphoric climate of sexual relationships. In "Ices Everlasting and Passions Perverted: The Physical and Moral Climates of Puig's Anti-Utopia," it is *Pubis Angelical* and especially its third part which is selected for extended examination. The cold, inhospitable physical climate becomes a metaphor for sterile and frigid human relationships. Prolonged sexual and economic exploitation of women (retrospectively depicted in Parts I and II) precede a cataclysmic alteration of Earth's climate to permanent polar winter, with the disappearance of human freedom and institutionalization of the enslavement and oppression seen as cyclic in earlier parts. Physical cold provides an allegory of male-female antagonism and predation.

Raquel Romeu examines the "Influence of Climate on the Cultures of the Jungle as Perceived by Two Latin American Novelists," i.e., Alejo Carpentier in *Los pasos perdidos* (*The Lost Steps*) and Mario Vargas Llosa in *El hablador* (*The Story-Teller*). Her approach emphasizes anthropological elements linked to climate in that they are peculiar to primitive cultures of the Amazon Basin portrayed in these novels. Carpentier depicts the Guahibo and Shirishana tribes, both living along tributaries of the Orinoco, while Vargas Llosa presents the Machiguenga from the Madre de Dios and upper Urubamba regions of the Amazon system. Both novels result from visits to the jungle and traverse different climates of the South American continent, suggesting the dependence of cultural development upon climate (civilization in the advanced, technological sense does not develop in jungle climates).

Jack Jordan in "Climate and Identity in the Literature of the French Antilles" examines the changing role played by climate in Francophone literature of the Caribbean from its beginnings in the Romantic-exotic period, through the Négritude movement in Guadeloupe and Martinique, to the third or Creole period. The Romantic period idealized climate, warm seas and marine zephyrs, overlooking the plight of enslaved blacks, while during the Négritude phase, West Indian "roots" were sought in a common black identity, African language and tribal customs, expressed by poets such as Aimé Césaire in Martinique. "Créolité" abjures "false universality, monolinguism and purity" and grounds itself in a dialectic established between nature and culture in the Caribbean—a cross-cultural poetics inseparable from the climate and landscape unique to the islands.

Luis A. Jiménez's interdisciplinary study of "Afro-Cuban Culture, Ecology and Climate in 'La comparsa' by Felipe Pichardo Moya" brings to bear a number of theorists of Afro-Cuban culture and adds sociological data on group dynamics, crowd behavior, and socio-cultural inhibition. Music, dance, voodoo rituals, and rum-drinking form part of the "ecosystem" of the *comparsa*, which is analyzed in accord with principles of community ecology. Via a close reading of the poem describing an orgiastic celebration, Jiménez underscores the interaction of climate, culture and ecology with kinetics and the atmosphere of the dance.

No single volume or series of volumes could do justice to the vastness of this topic, well-nigh inexhaustible. In bringing together this collection, we have sought essays which, by examining works across centuries, across oceans and genres, exemplify the myriad ways in which literature responds to environmental concerns (and anticipates them). Climates vary, but climate's ubiquity reminds us that the world is one.

Janet Pérez

 Writing the Bodies of Water:
The Clash of the Lasting and the
Catastrophic in the *Odes* of Horace.

Rosemary M. Nielsen and
Robert H. Solomon

Four times in *De Rerum Natura*,[1] Lucretius observes that terror and darkness of mind must be dispersed, not by rays of the sun or shining darts of the day, but by the "appearance" (*species*) and "order" (*ratio*) of nature. In the poem, order and appearance are not synonymous. While the permanence of the atom is actual, the orderliness and immutability of the external world of books and iron and sandstone are illusory. To Lucretius, the pre-Socratic elements of earth, air, fire, and water are not immutable, but, rather, "mortal" (cf. 5.238, *mortali corpore*); imbued with unsuspected vitality, they pass through changes of state, transformations approximating the death of the elements and transition to a re-birth in other forms. In Book 5, the dynamic, or "mortal," nature of elements may be recognized by intellection and intuitive poetic perception. Accepting Lucretius's witness undercuts the stability of the appearance of the physical world as Romans perceived it: if the four elements are not inviolate and independent and immortal, then physical stability only exists on the level of the invisible atom. Lucretius accepts that final atomist order and the accompanying reassurance, which is beneath direct experience and counter to intuition.

The unseen Lucretian dance of the "mortal" physical elements appears, for example, in Bailey's translation of 5,251 ff: "The earth, when baked by ceaseless suns, trodden by the force of many feet, gives off a mist and flying clouds of dust, which stormy winds scatter through all the air. Part too of its sods is summoned back to swamp by the rains, and streams graze and gnaw their banks.... For the rest, that sea, streams, and springs are ever filling with new moisture, and that waters are ceaselessly oozing forth, there is no need of words to prove . . ." (445). The motive force behind such elemental transformation is, as Bradley puts it, a "*vis abdita quaedam,* an irrational force, beyond calculation, and devoid of purpose" (321). The logic of elemental vitality is beyond man's comprehension, and the universe is a mosaic of irrational design at the level of the transitional elements; still, order is necessary to remove human fear. In Lucretius, physical borders of elements resemble the correct metrical patterns adopted in literature: both are necessary conventions, practical but not absolute truths.

Let us examine several implications of poetic images of a world in elemental transition in Horace's "Parade *Odes*";[2] the element in question is water. Our focus is not on the displacement of a stream-bank in spring floodtime, for example, nor on the vitality of wind or storm; it is on the change in water's physical state. By tracing this motif of the post-*semina* level of matter (the stratum above the primordial, atomic level), we may observe one way in which Horace incorporates Lucretian thought into his lyrics.

There are psychological and autobiographical causes for the appearance in Horace of many clusters of water images. Horace's native Apulia is a dry place, subject to flooding (*Odes* III.30.10 ff and IV.14.25 ff). Rivers, seas, and lakes are sometimes necessary to dramatic setting, but in the first nine odes, in particular, water occurs in all its forms, as cloud, rain, sea, mist, ice, frost, and snow; and, in each poem, transitions between states appear as central metaphors for the threats of chaos and catastrophe. In the modern, scientific sense of the last two terms, with which this study is concerned, "chaos" refers to a fall from a higher level of order to a lower one (as in a solution that passes the saturation point and ceases to accept dissolved particles); "catastrophe" signifies a cascading devolution (as in the event causing an irreversible movement from a stable bank of snow to an avalanche). Horace's "mortal" water carries philosophical resonances of Lucretius's poem.

Resonances of disorder and entropy are generated on several levels of existence in the odes and adhere to Horace's themes, themes that range from imperial politics, life's brevity, and fame's permanence to the vagaries and dangers of love. This metaphoric significance appears even in Book IV, where nature is not so frequently stage-center as it is in the early books.

For example, *Odes* IV.7 ("The snows have fled") presents a subtle version of Horace's concentration on man in a universe in flux, using the central trope of transition between forms of water: we look on snows as they disappear into meltwater (1-4), and on frosty coldness evaporating before west winds (9). The poem moves from snow and frost changing form to considerations of bodies changing state, crumbling to dust when we join rich

Tullus and Ancus and pious Aeneas in the Underworld (14-16). The fathers of classical civilization exist as shades but our bodies turn to earth. Elements disperse, interpenetrate,[3] and "die," much as mortal men do. The warfare between physical elements appears clearly in an earlier ode by Horace, I.11, where the border between water and land breaks, so that the Tyrrhenian seas are bitten back by the very cliffs they gnaw. States of being, like warring parts of the natural world, eat each other, as if to digest their opposites.

There are two basic, contrasting treatments of the fluid world in Horace's odes. In one water-motif, the borders are visible, physical places—rivers and seas that are named and described, and edges, that is, banks and cliffs that appear to be permanent. Though the borders may be violated, there is no interpenetration of physical states: the fluid's basic form, as liquid, gas, or solid, remains. In effect, the result is a basic landscape cluster and dramatic setting. In these descriptions, a river that overflows its banks remains a body of water, albeit in flood.

The difference between the types of water-images hinges on whether the border that defines states becomes indistinct. Whenever water evaporates or mixes with earth, rises as mist, or descends as snow, frost, or ice on the trees and streams of Mount Soracte in *Odes* I.9, we encounter the second image, the more frightening one of a sea-change to elements.

This second model of the fluid world presents water undergoing exchange of state, or threatening to do so. This is the imagery that we call, after Lucretius, "mortal" water; it challenges trust in secure borders; and when Horace uses it, deficits accrue on other levels. Mortal water accompanies physical danger, and, in addition, philosophical or religious confidence may be threatened, political power undercut, and sexual polarity challenged.

From the perspective of Horace's Rome, fearing renewed civil disturbances, foreign military involvements, and religious chaos of the sort Catullus presents in his "Attis" (Poem 63), flux threatens a new-won stability. Radical or unexpected change is inherently undesirable in urbanized society, where cooperation and control ensure what Thoreau (ironically) called "government . . . endeavouring to transmit itself unimpaired to posterity" (633). The collapse of the conventional boundaries and assumptions about the world may introduce a new plan that appears to be chaotic, that is, irrational by accepted standards of organized thought or action, and, therefore, in Lucretian terms, incomprehensible. Roman poets tie conventionality to sanity and order.

Catullus's Attis violates reasonable conduct. He is unmannered, alienated, and estranged from the pleasures of the Greek *polis* after sailing across wide waters—and religious and national borders—to worship Phrygian Cybele. Horace's motif of changes in water's physical state suggests an awareness of the possibility, especially during imperial consolidation, of renewed chaos on social, political, religious, and sexual scales. That concern inheres in human psychology; it is neither exclusively Roman nor specifically Horatian, for Lucretian motility of the elements overturns trust on a basic social and psychological level—if, to quote Robert Frost's carefully-blasted sonnet, "Design," "design govern in a thing so small" (as an individual's observations of the state of order in the natural world).

As Jurgens, Peitgen, and Saupe note in "The Language of Fractals," our scientific and mathematical communities are concerned with the chaotic and catastrophic beneath the apparently stable and orderly, but with dissimilar motivations and results from those we posit for Horace's day. Physics rests now on an invisible world of counter-intuitive patterns—subatomic quarks and leptons, cosmological black holes and central attractors, and universal quantum mechanical states. "[F]ractal geometry is the geometry of chaos" (60). By means of algebra and algorithms, mathematicians using high-speed computation investigate the statistical representation of chaos and catastrophe, creating mathematical models to explain changes in states of being. Similarly, Mandelbrot and others employ fractal equations to probe seemingly unpredictable phenomena (e.g. atmospheric turbulence). "Once one has a command of the fractal language, one can describe the shape of a cloud as precisely . . . as an architect might describe a house with blueprints that use the language of traditional geometry" (61).

This is not Horace's world-picture. While Lucretius cogitates on elemental physical disorder, the mathematics and religion of his day (and Horace's) lack theoretical space for assimilating chaos and catastrophe as mere abstractions. As a consequence, whenever Horace contemplates the Lucretian picture of un- stable states of a "mortal" element, fear and shock reverberate through the poem.

The modifications in scientific context are fascinating to ponder in terms of the evolution of metaphor. But literary observations by Bachelard, who is a historian of science as well as a critic, may be more useful to our present study than the mathematics of Mandelbrot and the physics of Heisenberg. Bachelard's *The Poetics of Space* describes the "havens" within which individuality is nurtured. The spaces may be actual corners of rooms or houses, or images in dreams or poems. They ensure psychological safety, from which to meditate on "immensity" and "intimacy" (183-212). Bachelard believes that poets express the quest for such corners by means of figures of minimal containment of space; he identifies geometrical elements, in particular the triangle, that are reassuring spaces. The triangle represents the least number of straight lines necessary for enclosure. Coveting firm borders, every person, artist or not, and every society, reveres and encloses space, personal or public, as if it were almost "sacred." In Eliade's anthropology, one "wedges himself into Being" (32) by entering sacred places and rituals.

Order implies its opposite: in the world in which Horace wrote, as Mills says of Virgil, "Anything out of the ordinary . . . belongs to the realm of the unpredictable and chaotic" (34). According to L'Orange, the goal of Roman art and religion was a "static world of types and eternal orders . . ." (129). We believe that Horace senses the Roman "rage for order," and the corollary fear of order's end in lesser organization, chaos, or final dissolution of recognizable pattern, catastrophe.

The notion of securely enclosed space is essential to our understanding of Horace's metaphors of water in transition; it is also important in Lucretius, who combines the triangle, secure borders, and the threat of water-in-transition (*DRN* I, 715 ff.) when he describes Empedocles (733, "scarce born of human stock") by placing imagery of space-closure and geometric terms against a transitional or interpenetrative elemental setting: "him that island bore within the three-cornered coasts of its lands, around which flows the Ionian ocean, with many a winding inlet, splashing salt foam from its green waves, while with narrow strait a tearing sea sunders with its waves the coasts of Aeolia's lands from the island-borders" (Bailey 213). The safety of triangular space is impeached by the gnawing element of water—the triangle, central to Roman ballistics (Marsden 24-85), navigation (Casson 77-96, 141-82), architecture and construction (Vitruvius 201), is dissolving.

From the perspective of man's search for the comforts inherent in stable borders between inside and outside, the number of images of fluid borders in the odes suggests that Horace (who never uses explicit words for "chaos" in these poems) is investigating the consequences, social and psychological, as well as religious, of Roman belief in strict order. The fluid borders occur in poems about unpredictable Days (I.4 & IV.7), and unknowable Tomorrows (I.9 & 11); they also appear in poems like I.5, the Pyrrha *Ode,* in which men who think they know for certain what is masculine and feminine fall victim to their inflexible definitions of the two sexes. The prime example of a simplistic reader of womankind may be the "youth" (1, *puer*), who is undone amid dripping, not evaporating, scent. Beginning with *Odes* I.2., we can watch Horace's two types of water-imagery diverge, with the clashing of states and collapsing of borders always accompanying primal fears and darkness of mind, Lucretius's description of man's sense of universal disorder.

I.2 begins with a winter scene. Michie translates it: "Enough the ordeal now, the snow-and-hail-storms/God has unleashed on earth, whose red right hand hurled/bolts at the Capitol's sacred summits, spreading/Fear in the streets" (5). The Latin opens with "*Iam satis terris nivis*" (1), and after a flood of sybillants, ends "*arces/terruit urbem*" (3-4). The second stanza repeats "*terruit*"(5), the similarity of sounds in "*terris*" and "*terruit*" tying the word for fear to that for the earth itself. Then the poem shifts to what Michie calls "the whole sea-zoo" of Proteus's playful seals marooned on the mountaintops (5-8), and moves, in the third stanza, to the race of fish peopling the trees (9-10): the scene of this ode is the all-engulfing primeval flood, "*superiecto . . . / aequore*" (11-12).

Beyond question, things in the natural world of I.2 appear topsy-turvy. The inversion of earth and sea contrasts with the poem's praise for the political order of Rome: as Commager describes it, the ode reveals the "gap" that remains between "temporal and eternal rule[s]" (176). Notwithstanding the truth of Wickham's estimation of the poem as "palinode and 'apologia'" (38), I.2 is, as in Commager's playful description, "something more than a weather report" (179). The conflict between physical climate and political climate is instructive, for the poem's cluster of father-leader images (which exists alongside its descriptions of aberrant nature), offers male, indeed patriarchal, confidence to offset, though not to cure, chaotic nature.[4] The simplistic solution is not typical of the poems in which Horace writes of mortal water, and, on close examination, the motif is missing.

The aberrance of I.2 lacks a philosophical-psychological threat inherent in "mortal" (lit., "death-bound") water; instead of discovering interpenetrating states of water, we observe a body of water merely placed into the wrong geographical context. The water is displaced, but it is not disappearing, nor is it "dying," as Lucretius describes it, to be reborn in another form. The flood is a natural accident in a dangerous world: even in floodtide, the water is the water is the water, as Gertrude Stein might have put it.

There is physical danger, nevertheless, as the Tiber overflows in the poem; its movement to the left is sinister in the fourth stanza, where it threatens Vesta and her temple, as well as King Numa's palace. But I.2 ends with the flooding sea removed from stage center. The land's borders are restored, and the heavens quieted: chaos is avoided, and the escape from natural danger is celebrated with the famous magisterial salute "with you as leader, Caesar" (52, *te duce, Caesar*). Rome can control flood waters, seems the message.

By turning the land-world momentarily into a comic, complete sea-cosmos, Horace actually forecloses the possibility of interpenetration and metamorphosis between water-states. There is no mist, no cloud of spray, no melted ice, no land's edge bitten and digested by seas; there is no change to the state of water. That element is unruly in quantity and placement, but it is not unstable in form or vitality.

To see the second imagery of water, and to observe the elemental drift from stability, we must move past the next two poems, I.3 and I.4. The third Parade *Ode* praises seamen who shall prosper from good winds amid sea-monsters, while their boat bears Vergil to Attica. The poem celebrates epic conventions and Horace calls Vergil "half my soul" (Michie 9): and although the four winds contend, water stays separate from the winds, an unchanging entity, as in I.2.

Odes I.4 displays shifting seasons; amid references to Hades, Vulcan's heated forge, and the beating steps of "the Death-Goddess" (13, *Pallida Mors*), the water, however, remains constant. Wine and springtime bounty provide nurture and a sense, albeit illusory, of stability. There are resonances of winter in the ode's spring: sacrifices to the fertility god, Faunus (11-12), and the Underworld with its coterie of "storied shades" (16). After the warm winds (1, *Favoni*) return, and under a looming or portent-filled moon, the white covering of the green meadows dissolves (4). The moment of vernal change flashes past; Horace does not concentrate on the transition of water from snow to cold air, cold stream, and spring rains. Although Death haunts the spring, adding an eerie note of mortality, it is not the Lucretian dying of the physical elements. Human mortality can appear without that added resonance, sorrow without elemental disorder.

Thus the first poem to exploit fully the second motif, of changing water-states, is I.5. The initial piece in the mosaic introduces liquid at the moment of evaporation. The scene is reported through rhetorical questions, almost unanswerable in the context in which they appear. "What slim youth," the speaker asks, "dripping scent, urges love on you, Pyrrha, amid roses in some cave?" To woo Pyrrha, the *puer* has chosen liquid perfume, a gloss that, in his excess of bad taste and ardor, has turned to (or remained) a dripping liquid. It has resisted complete evaporation or sublimated back in the heated, and certainly humid, atmosphere of the love-grotto. This change of condition of a fluid bespeaks a physical world's betrayal of a young man's love-plans. In its simplemindedness, the *puer*'s confidence in observing the courting conventions matches his trust in the predictability of basic physical phenomena. His perfume is supposed to disappear as it evaporates: to atomize, so that Pyrrha will be joined to him. The youth is confident in other stabilities that are illusory—he believes that Pyrrha will remain "empty" (10, *vacuam*), as well as "open to love-exchanges" (*amabilem*). She will be neither; and the next image of the *puer,* following his perfume's confused states of being and Pyrrha's confounding state of readiness, is of a male lost amid "black winds" (7, *nigris . . . ventis*) and "savage seas" (6-7, *asperal . . . aequora*). His mistaken belief in social order and literary convention dissolves in an atmosphere of water in mortal, and not merely physical, motion. That interpenetration symbolizes the mortality of elemental fluids: sea merges with wind to form wet storm-winds. Water, perfume, and conventional love-motifs—these are impermanent forms in *De Rerum Natura* and *Odes* I.5, flux-driven and fluid.

The final image of water assigned to the *puer* consists of salt tears shed at his fate. Like Lucretius's sea gnawing the solid land of Empedocles's Sicily, the watery tears of the *puer* carry away the body they touch. Upon evaporation, some bit of the *puer* will undergo metamorphosis. Like sea-cliffs eroded by sea-water, and sea that touches stormwinds, his body, in the form of salt, enters, penetrates the elemental borders of water; and then it enters the air. One word-choice carries the notion of fluidity of borders: with the modifier *aspera, aequora* suggests, not "layers" or "depths" of water, but, rather, the "face" of waves—the "countenance," the conventional border that dissolves and becomes unrecognizable, one assumes, as sea, wind, cloud, and spray merge and re-emerge. I.5 ends with the narrator's votive offering: he proffers it with water, not perfume, dripping from his clothes. After images of interpenetrating water, the speaker stands, probably stripped, naked—a parody of the frustrated love-dreams of the illusion-draped youth and "those doomed in love," the *miseri* (12).

This poem thus presents the chief characteristics of Horace's motif of "mortal" water. At the elemental level, nature becomes unexpectedly untrustworthy; men are deceived by the appearance of basic order. Conventional truths about water, perfume, and woman's nature are illusions, no matter what Romans accept as tradition, intuition, and belief. This ode, too, is more than a weather report! When catastrophe is averted, salvation comes, but only for the narrator, not for the *miseri* or the *puer;* and it arrives by virtue of divine and not human intervention. One fact emerges as the man hangs his votive plate (13-14, *tabula . . . / votiva*), and perhaps his dripping clothes on the poem's only stable physical construction, which is the last panel's sacred wall (*sacer / . . . paries*): that god is *potenti . . . / deo* (15-16). Powerful, it is also unapproachable: one cannot know whether it is Neptune or Venus (Fredricksmeyer). The poem brings the reader from over-confidence in gender-borders to good-humoured uncertainty.

Limitations on space do not permit us to discuss every water-cluster in the odes. But in *Odes* I.7, Horace approaches the second water-motif: celebrating his humble origins and poetic goals. As Michie translates it, the speaker draws a picture of cascading water, southern winds, and orchard rivulets in his homeland's dance of irrigation (12-14). Winds blow away the clouds and do "not breed rains" (15-17). The ode completes its mosaic of juxtaposed elements with the story of Teucer who is embarking upon his father-ordered exile. Wine and camaraderie fill the final lines—nature, man, and the elements are under control, within borders, restoring the appearance of order.

Resonances of elemental disorder, nevertheless, persist: by implication, the rains could have come from the clouds, water rising to fill them before plunging to earth, and the poem echoes with the disorder of Troy, the death of Ajax, a son's body alleged to have been neglected by his half-brother,[5] and images of exile and possible death. Once more, however, the primal waters remain within bounds. Elemental chaos is averted.

The next ode, I.8, is a series of questions to Lydia about her affect on Sybaris, and it examines the polarities inherent in the Roman construct of manliness, a cluster of conventions which does not match the complicated reality of male response in love. The definition, the border, of a man proves insufficient. The poem depends on elemental transitions in state to dramatize the error of sexual polarization, but the mortal element is not water. The movement in the poem's setting is from the heat-baked exercise ground, or earthen plain (4, *campum*), where Sybaris used to play, to dust (*pulveris*). Sybaris himself loses the virile body of an athlete to become a mere analogy to a skulking, fearful Achilles: in addition, Sybaris, forgetting athlete's oil, hides unbruised and dry. Interpenetration of the states of mortal elements appears in the "dying" of the earth (a fluidity appropriate to a poem about a man no longer on firm ground). He is as undone by blind faith in social conventions as the over-done *puer* was in I.5. The resonances are surprisingly similar to those accompanying mortal water, although Horace here presents the earth as the fluid element.

The final Parade *Ode*, I.9, returns us to the instability of physical states of water, amid evanescent climate. The famous Soracte *Ode* opens with that snowy mountain viewed from afar, rivers frozen solid, bent trees groaning as they struggle to free themselves of snowy burdens (1-4). The second stanza contains the well-known injunction to dissolve the cold, fill the fireplace with logs—and pour four-year old Sabine wine—as if human efforts could restore earth's warmth or forestall spring flooding from melting ice and snow.

Then there is a sudden shift to a spring storm or an autumn one (9-12), while ash-trees and cypress, species associated with mourning (11-12), seek safety amid contesting winds and tempestuous ocean waves. Thus, although winter retreats, safety is unassured, because storm-winds and sea merge in the second season as in the first. As a consequence, the primary borders between water-states continue to disappear even after winter ends: waters "die," changing state of being, to be "reborn" as a second dangerous climate. The reader's initial perceptions of an orderly seasonal progression prove incorrect, and one is left uncertain of which season the poet describes (Cunningham and Sullivan). But whatever the new time of year, the storm of interpenetration threatens chaos. We find unpredictability and a second mode of death for trees. The poem has drawn the reader past the groaning trees and cracking ice on the streams, past vernal splendor, past man-made heat—only to encounter an equally threatening mosaic of storm. In the Soracte *Ode,* the mortality of elemental borders redoubles the threat inherent in the climate, challenging our faith that other seasons lack winter's deadliness. The poem suggests, instead, that the world will not be safe—like Pyrrha, its elements disappoint our expectations. Horace presents hard-edged ice and snow-burden, something every Italian fears, whether from nearby (or on Mt. Soracte) or far away; and the storm reveals a second chaotic climate. The third or final threatening climate consists of the dissolving boundaries to water; dangerous climates may be seasonal or elemental.

Like the seasons and their climates, Fortune's gifts cannot be counted in advance, but must be recorded as they are measured out (13-15). Security is missing, if water kills as heavy snow and ice, and again as wet storm-winds, but, in an unpredictable lifetime, the addition of elemental disorderliness may be unbearable. Once recognized, the illusory nature of elemental borders enriches our reading of Horace's poems, especially the "Parade *Odes.*"

These representative poems present the two basic motifs for water in Horace's four books. Later, in III.1, for example, we see the first type again: in that poem, fish are imprisoned by piers erected under a villa: man invading water, with his bronze-beaked trireme and ostentatious villa, bears personified Fear, Forebodings, and Care (33-40). But the borders he transgresses are those of good taste and respect for the natural environment. Missing, however, is the motif of elemental mortality.

In III.30, Horace speculates, in fact, that only poetry has safe borders—a shape that angry winds and biting rains may not erode (3-5), a convention that poets from Shakespeare to Wallace Stevens have utilized. But in many of the poems of Horace, stability and permanence are doubted, and the motif of elemental fluidity is never far away, contending for primacy with the first picture of water, as mere setting.

This struggle between the two water-motifs occurs in the lines of a poet who recognizes Lucretian vitality. Although Horace also reacts to the actual physical climates he knows—of Apulia, Sicily, Rome, and Soracte, his poetic world is an invented one. It is a compound, an interpenetration of metaphor and description. The American poet, Wallace Stevens, also focuses on the interplay of philosophical and physical climates, as well as on the interplay between imagery as recreation of detail and as revelation or vision. In "Description of Place" (339-46), Stevens explores poetic principles that lie behind Horace's water-motifs: "Description" he writes, "is revelation. It is not / The thing described, nor false facsimile" (121-22). He continues, as Horace might have: "Thus the theory of description matters most. / It is the theory of the word for those / For whom the word is the making of the world"

(133-135). Horace makes the world, in part, from clusters of water-descriptions. He reveals two motifs for this aspect of natural, or external, and philosophical-psychological, or internal, climates. Horace leaves lyric poetry as a paradox: "a monument more lasting than bronze", (III.30.1, *monumentum aere perennius*), but resonating with images of evanescent, untrustworthy, frightening, and instructive "mortal" water.

Notes

1. 1,146ff; 2,59ff; 3,91ff; 6,39ff. Unless otherwise noted, all translations of the Latin are our own.
2. A title given to the first nine poems of Book I for their marshalling of diverse meters and subjects. Cf. Dettmer's useful schemata of eighteen interlocking rings of themes in Books I-III (531-41).
3. Further on interpenetrating seasons and states of water in *Odes* IV.7, see our "Horace and Housman" (329-35).
4. Quinn traces a pattern of "portents" in stanza 1, "cataclysms" in stanzas 2-3, and, in the final stanzas, "consequences of the unreasoning, destructive pursuit of revenge" (122).
5. On Horace's bold variation of the Teucer myth, see Nisbett and Hubbard, *passim* (90-108).

Works Cited

Bachelard, Gaston. *The Poetics of Space.* Trans. Maria Jolas. Boston: Beacon Press, 1969.
Bailey, Cyril. *Titi Lucreti Cari. De Rerum Natura*, Vol. I. Oxford: Clarendon Press, 1947.
Bradley, Edward, M. "Lucretius and the Irrational." *Classical Journal* 67 (1972): 317-22.
Casson, Lionel. *Ships and Seamanship in the Ancient World.* Princeton: Princeton University Press, 1973.
Commager, Steele. *The Odes of Horace. A Critical Study.* New Haven: Yale University Press, 1962.
Cunningham, M. P. "*Enarratio* of Horace's *Odes* I, 9." *Classical Philology* 52 (1967): 98-102.
Dettmer, Helena. *Horace. A Study in Structure.* Hildesheim: Olms-Weidmann, 1983.
Eliade, M. *Patterns in Comparative Religion.* Trans. Rosemary Sheed. Cleveland: Meridian, 1958.
Fredricksmeyer, Ernest A. "Horace, *Odes,* I.5,16: God or Goddess?" *Classical Philology* 67 (1972): 124-26.
Jurgens, Helmut, Heinz-Otto Peitgen, and Dietmar Saupe. "The Language of Fractals." *Scientific American* 263 (Aug. 1990): 60-67.
L'Orange, H. P. *Art Forms and Civic Life in the Late Roman Empire.* Princeton: Princeton University Press, 1972.
Marsden, E. W. *Greek and Roman Artillery: Historical Development.* Oxford: Clarendon Press, 1969.
Michie, James. *The Odes of Horace.* New York: Washington Square Press, Inc., 1965.
Mills, Donald H. "'Sacred Space' in Vergil's *Aeneid.*" *Vergilius* 29 (1983): 34-46.

Nielsen, Rosemary M., and Robert H. Solomon. "Horace and Houseman: Twisting Conventions." *Canadian Review of Comparative Literature* 13 (1986): 325-49.

Nisbet, R. G. M., and M. Hubbard. *A Commentary on Horace: Odes I*. Oxford: Oxford University Press, 1970.

Quinn, Kenneth. *The Odes of Horace*. London: St. Martin's Press, 1980.

Stevens, Wallace. *Wallace Stevens. The Collected Poems*. New York: Vintage Press, 1982.

Sullivan, G. S. "Horace: *Odes* I.9." *American Journal of Philology* 84 (1963): 290-94.

Thoreau, Henry David. *Walden and Other Writings*. Ed. William Howarth. New York: Random House, 1981.

Vitruvius. *De Architectura. Books VI-X*. 2 vols. Trans. F. Granger. Loeb Classical Library. Cambridge, Mass.: Harvard University Press, 1970.

Wickham, E. C. *The Works of Horace*. Vol. I. Oxford: Clarendon Press, 1896.

 Climate as Science and Metaphor in the Writings of Jehuda Halevi

Stephen T. Newmyer

Zionism, the quest of Jews to return from dispersion at the corners of the earth to true Jewish life in the Holy Land, is most frequently viewed exclusively in its essentially nineteenth century political guise and is almost invariably linked with Theodor Herzl's efforts to reestablish a Jewish homeland in Palestine. Yet the desire of Jews to resettle in the Holy Land is as old as the destruction of Jerusalem by the Babylonians in 587 B.C., the event that gave birth to the Jewish Diaspora and that was lamented already in the words of the author of Psalm 137:

> If I forget you, O Jerusalem,
> let my right land wither away;
> let my tongue cling to the roof of my mouth
> if I do not remember you,
> if I do not set Jerusalem
> above my highest joy.

In the centuries that intervened between the Babylonian Exile and the foundation of the modern Jewish State, Jews developed various arguments advancing the position that observant Jewish life was possible only in the Holy Land. One of the most fervent supporters of this notion was the medieval Jewish philosopher-physician-poet Jehuda Halevi of Toledo (ca. 1080-1140). While Halevi's importance as a precursor of Zionist thinking is widely acknowledged, certain aspects of his arguments for the need for a return to Zion have escaped the notice of scholars. This study discusses Halevi's use of some elements of Jewish scientific, in particular climatological, thought to inspire in his readers a fervent desire to return to the Jewish homeland. It will argue that Halevi's scientific pronouncements are derived from the medical lore of the Talmud, which may in turn be influenced by classical Greek climatological thinking. The idea which Halevi especially emphasizes is the peculiarly salutary effect of the climate of the Holy Land upon the people who inhabit it which renders it, he claims, especially suitable as the site for a restored Jewish community.

The Talmud has been called the portable home of the Jews. An immense compilation of oral commentary on the Hebrew Bible, it contains legal ordinances (*halakhah*) and storylike material (*haggadah*) which are called together the *mishnah*, or "review," and which interpret the meaning of the Scriptures for everyday Jewish living. Amassed over hundreds of years following the codification of the Scriptures and including the debates of hundreds of Rabbis, the materials of this "Oral Torah" were edited around the year A.D. 200 by Rabbi Judah ha-Nasi, who feared that soon no one would be able to retain in his head the huge amount of orally-transmitted debate and discussion. In time, commentary on the *mishnah*, called *gemara*, was added to the *mishnah*, and they form together the Talmud. Because a number of rabbinic scholars whose opinions contributed to the Talmud were practicing physicians and because of the practical need to determine by medical means the suitability of animals for human consumption, the Talmud is full of medical lore, some of it remarkable advanced in outlook.

The origins of Talmudic medical knowledge remain obscure for a number of reasons. Most importantly, the Talmudists are curiously reticent concerning their sources, particularly when non-Jewish sources may be suspected. While one is frequently struck by the similarity between a rabbinic medical idea and a classical Greek idea, the only pagan writers mentioned by name in the Talmud are Homer, Epicurus and Oenomaus of Gadara, and none of these is mentioned in a scientific context. Scholars eager to argue that the Talmudic Rabbis were not attracted to pagan science quote the familiar rabbinic pronouncement (Baba Batra 82b), "Cursed be the man who would breed swine and cursed be the man who would teach his son Grecian Wisdom."[1] Yet there is clear evidence in the Talmud that the Rabbis were in fact attracted to "Grecian Wisdom." The scientific vocabulary of the Talmud reveals over one hundred words in the areas of anatomy, illness, medicines and the work of the physician which are derived from Greek.[2] Especially significant in this context, however, is a discussion (Pesahim 94b) of Jewish and gentile opinions on the question of the movement of celestial bodies. The Rabbis are quoted as arguing that the sun travels beneath the sky by day and above it by night while the gentiles hold that the sun travels beneath the sky by day and below the earth by night. Rabbi Judah ha-Nasi remarks in this passage on these contrasting ideas, ". . . and their view is preferable to ours, for the wells are cold by day and warm by night."

The Talmud formed the basis of study for Jews living in the Diaspora who were eager to conduct their lives in full accord with Jewish law, and its pronouncements, though a thousand years old in Halevi's time, were considered to be the living word of God's most inspired sages. No matter where a Jewish community was located, possession of the Talmud allowed Jews to feel themselves in contact with the Holy Land. Halevi, as a member of the active Jewish community of Spain, was intimately familiar with the Talmud and, as a physician, was particularly attracted by the medical doctrine of the Talmudists.

The Talmud is a product of the exile of the Jews from their homeland, for the longer recension of the text was prepared in Babylonia. Consequently, it is deeply imbued with the longing for return and the sadness of separation from the land which are so characteristic of early literary manifestations of Zionist thinking. Gerson Cohen, in his article "Zionism in Rabbinic Literature," has written of the profound attachment which the Talmudists felt to their lost spiritual homeland, "We do less than justice to Rabbinic Judaism, if we do not stress the inseverable connection it had with the land of Israel not only ideologically, but quite practically and legally. The Rabbis could no more conceive of Judaism without the *land* of Israel than they could have without the *people* of Israel."[3] Those Rabbis who continued to dwell in Palestine, whose pronouncements also found their way into the Talmud, faced a different problem from those in the Diaspora. For many centuries after the Babylonian Exile, Palestine was in the hands of foreign governments whose oppressive taxation and harsh rule prompted many Jews to seek relief in emigration from Palestine, prompting the Rabbis, who were the spiritual guides of Jewish communities in Palestine and in the Diaspora, to fear the depopulation of Palestine. It is in the light of this very practical consideration that one must view some rabbinic pronouncements on the special status of Palestine against its neighboring nations. When the Rabbis praise the purity of the air of the Holy Land, their motivation may in fact be more economic than scientific. Yet one can find already in the books of the Bible traces of the notion that the Holy Land is to be set against other nations, as in Joshua 22:19, "If the land you have taken is unclean, then cross over to the Lord's own land."

As centuries passed and return to Zion became impractical or impossible, the real harshness of life in the Holy Land receded from the memory of Jews, and the economic motivation for some rabbinic claims on the preferability of the Holy Land was forgotten. Only the grandeur of Zion remained. Chaim Dimitrovsky, in his article "Zion in Medieval Literature," has well characterized this remarkable transformation, specifically as it influenced the post-rabbinic attitude toward Jerusalem, "The physical Jerusalem in all its glory became more and more idealized; its earthly, historical reality receded and grew vague, and it was replaced by an idealized conception incorporating all that was noble and lofty. And out of their love for it the people added to it innumerable nuances of beauty and splendor."[4]

In no Jewish writer of the medieval period does this somewhat romanticized view of Zion appear more gloriously than in Halevi, who wrote in one of his poems, "Beautiful light! O Joy! The whole world's gladness! O great King's city, mountain blest! My soul is yearning unto thee—is yearning from limits of the west."[5] In Halevi's view, Jewish exile in Spain was painful because it forced the Jew to spread God's message from lands where it was not meant to be centered. Prophecy, Judaism's role, was possible only in Zion. Hence, the pious Jew must renounce exile and return to Zion, as indeed Halevi did at the end of his life. Halevi's fervor for return to Zion is the more remarkable when it is seen against the solutions to the problem of exile offered by some of his near-contemporaries. While the medieval period did witness the appearance of numerous individuals who claimed to be the Messiah and who promised to restore Zion to Jewish hands, Halevi's famous compatriot Moses Maimonides (1135-1204), like Halevi a physician as well as a philosopher, held that the possession of Torah was the essential fact of Judaism, and that therefore true Jewish life was possible in study of Scripture. Not only was return to Zion not necessary, Maimonides argued, but life there would require so many observances that one would not have time for the study of Torah, which was the Jew's highest duty.

Halevi, in contrast, felt that the realization of God's ancient covenant between Himself and the Jews required a physical location for fulfillment, and that that location was Palestine, the only place where the divine could manifest itself. This notion is central to the argument of Halevi's greatest work, the *Kuzari*, which he subtitled "A Defense of a Despised Religion," some of whose own adherents, he noted, scorned it. The *Kuzari* is unique in medieval Jewish literature in being the only extended philosophical work cast in the form of a dialogue. The setting of the work recalls a famous legend of Jewish history. Around A.D. 740, Bulan, King of the Khazars in southern Russia, converted his people to Judaism after examining the doctrine of the Christian, Islamic and Jewish religions. The tribe retained its allegiance to Judaism into the thirteenth century.

According to Halevi's account in the *Kuzari*, the King of the Khazars had a dream in which an angel informed him that his thought was pleasing to God but not his actions, so he inquired of a philosopher the nature of correct religion. His abstract account of the operation of the world, in particular his claim that God neither created man nor concerns Himself with man, disappointed the King, but before he disappears from the dialogue the philosopher utters a statement which curiously foreshadows Halevi's upcoming use of climatological arguments for the excellence of Palestine. Indeed, the philosopher might have had the Hippocratic treatise *Airs Waters Places* in mind when he reflects (I. 1), ". . . There never arose a man otherwise than through one who came into existence before him, in whom were united forms, gifts, and characteristics inherited from father, mother, and other relations, besides the influences of climate, countries, foods and water, spheres, stars and constellations."[6]

After dismissing the philosopher, the King of the Khazars inquired of a Doctor of Islamic Philosophy and of a Christian Scholastic as to what pleased God. He notes that he will not bother to consult any Jews since they are of low station, being few in number and generally despised by the world. Surprisingly, both the Scholastic and the Arab freely acknowledge that they are the intellectual children of Israel. The King is therefore moved to conclude (I. 10), "Indeed, I see myself compelled to ask the Jews, because they are the relic of the children of Israel. For I see that they constitute in themselves the evidence for the divine law on earth."[7]

In the course of five lengthy discussions, the Rabbi whom the King consults argues that the genius of Judaism consists not in its rationality, as some contemporary apologists for the faith had held, but rather in its unique historical position as a faith made true by direct election by God. Only the Jew, as God's elect, can properly understand the religious life. Yet Halevi is careful not to insult the rival religions with his doctrine of chosenness, arguing that Christianity and Islam have a part to play in history and will in time be brought back to Judaism. If the history of Judaism is unique, so is the stage upon which it acts out its history: the Holy Land. Halevi taught that God strove to raise men to Himself by implanting in them a non-rational religious faculty which gives rise to a yearning to be with God. This union can be effected, in accordance with God's ordinance, only in the Holy Land. Indeed, the faculty resides only in Jews and the union it promises is accomplished by correct observance of ceremonial law and ritual, a process which can be achieved only in the Holy Land and only in the Hebrew language.

After the Rabbi has set forth the special nature of Judaism in the first section of the dialogue, he remarks at the beginning of the second section that the workings of God's attributes can be observed only in the Holy Land (II. 8), "Even so does the glory of God ... benefit His people in His country."[8] The King then asks what the Rabbi means by "His country," and the Rabbi's response offers a first instance of Halevi's use of climatological argumentation in his portrait of the Holy Land. "Thou wilt have no difficulty in perceiving," the Rabbi replies (II. 10), "that one country may have higher qualifications than others. There are places in which particular plants, metals, or animals are found, or where the inhabitants are distinguished by their form and character, since perfection or deficiency of the soul are produced by the mingling of the elements."[9] The reason why this excellence is to be found in Palestine, the Rabbi explains, is that the divine influence is preeminent there. That is why Jewish heroes have always sought to be inside, rather than outside, Palestine. Yet Halevi's notion that some lands produce especially excellent plants, animals and metals will recall at once to the student of ancient medicine the idea, formulated at length first in the Hippocratic treatise *Airs Waters Places* and repeated with variations throughout antiquity, that some climates are preferable to others, to such an extent that they even produce superior physical and intellectual capabilities in their inhabitants. The Hippocratic author had used this idea to argue that Europeans are physically and mentally superior to Asians because the climate of Europe is more varied and free of extremes than that of Asia (*Airs Waters Places* XII). When the Romans took up this notion, they were able to pinpoint Rome as having the world's most salutary climate. The architect Vitruvius, writing in the first century A.D., could conclude with some satisfaction (*De Architectura* VI.1.11), "Thus the divine mind has allotted to the Roman state an excellent and temperate region in order to rule the world."[10] This search for the ideal climate, which is so closely influenced by feelings of national pride, reappears in the Talmud, in an interesting transformation, where it is argued that the climate of the Holy Land is the healthiest on earth.[11] Because it was felt that the Holy Land was physically more elevated than neighboring nations, the Rabbis argued that corpses did not decompose so rapidly there as outside the Holy Land, and tractate Ketuboth (111a) goes so far as to claim, in a manner recalling our passage in Halevi, that Palestine produces larger cabbages than grow elsewhere!

While the debt to Talmudic climatology may be only slightly felt in this passage of the Kuzari, Halevi soon becomes explicit in his borrowings. When the King asks to hear the reasons why Palestine is held in such high regard by so many peoples, the Rabbi begins (II. 22) by observing that it is preferable to dwell in the Holy Land in a town inhabited by heathens than to dwell in a town abroad inhabited by Jews. He then proceeds to quote several Talmudic regulations concerning the special nature of the Holy Land, ending with the comment, "Further, the atmosphere of the Holy Land makes wise."[12] This is almost a quote from tractate Baba Batra 158b, where a famous debate is recounted, the point of which is to prove that the very atmosphere of the Holy Land is superior. We are told there that on one occasion Rabbi Zera, who dwelled in the Diaspora in Babylon, and Rabbi Elai, a Palestinian, were engaged in a debate over who should inherit the family estate if a house collapsed on a man and on his mother. Rabbi Elai insisted that the heirs of the son should inherit while Rabbi Elai insisted that the heirs of the mother inherit. When Rabbi Zera came to Palestine, however, he adopted Rabbi Elai's opinion. The *gemara* on the passage draws the interesting conclusion, "From this one may deduce that the climate of the land of Israel makes one wise." The pious Jew, in whom Halevi sought to inspire a longing to return to the Holy Land, would have been likely, on reading this Talmudic reminiscence, to recall other Talmudic pronouncements on the health-giving air of the Holy Land. He would recall, for instance, that cinnamon logs were burned in Jerusalem for fuel, and that their fragrance was said to pervade all of Israel (Shabbat 63a), and he would recall the anecdote (Ketuboth 104a) that, since elevated locations are especially salubrious, one Jewish sage was sent to the lofty Palestinian town of Sepphoris to breathe its health-restoring air. Much care was taken in Palestine to prevent air pollution by industry. Tractate Baba Batra 26b recounts that carrion animals, graves and tanyards had to be kept fifty cubits from Palestinian towns because of their noxious fumes. Likewise, threshing floors were to be kept fifty cubits from towns lest their chaff damage health.

While it is impossible to know to what extent such hyperbolic claims for the peculiar excellence of the climate of the Holy Land may reflect rabbinic desire to emulate classical formulations of the climatological superiority of the Greco-Roman world noted above, Halevi is clearly aware of the Greek scientific tradition, for he compares it to Talmudic scientific thinking in the fourth section of the Kuzari, finding Talmudic science superior even to Galen. The Rabbi begins his discussion of Talmudic science by stating (IV. 29), "The remarkable knowledge of natural history displayed in the sayings of the Sages . . . is quite astonishing."[13] Unfortunately, the Rabbi laments, the anatomical and medical handbooks which the Talmudists produced are lost, for when a nation perishes, its literature perishes first. He continues (IV. 31), "There only remain the law books which the people require, know by heart, copy and preserve. Whatever element of those sciences was embodied in Talmudical law codes was thus protected and preserved by the zeal of many students. To these belong everything appertaining to the rules for slaughtering cattle, or making them unlawful to be eaten. A large amount of this remained unknown to Galen."[14] It is not accident that Galen is mentioned here. As the agent through whose writings the best of Greek science passed to the Middle Ages, Galen was a writer studied avidly by medieval Jewish physicians. It was through Galen's writings that Hippocratic climatological thinking could have reached Talmudic scientists, for he elaborated the doctrine of the *Airs Waters Places* in his treatise entitled *That Mental Faculties Follow the Bodily Constitution*. Moreover, Galen's doctrine that all things in nature are designed by God to function in the best possible manner toward the end for which they were designed proved immensely attractive to Jewish scholars, and in the final section of the *Kuzari* (V. 8), Halevi praises Galen for it.[15] The purposeful teleology of Galen's world view is quoted by Halevi to prove the Psalmist's observation (Psalm 104: 24), "How great are Thy works, O Lord." Perhaps by mentioning Galen here, Halevi is acknowledging that he is aware of the debt of the Talmudists to Greek thinking, not least in the use of Greek doctrine that some climates are superior to others.

The greatest of the Lord's works, in Halevi's view, is Zion, and his *Kuzari* bristles with Talmudic reminiscences designed to support this idea. Of these the climatological arguments for the excellence of Zion examined in this study form but a small part. Unlike many visionaries, Halevi took his own advice and returned to Zion. According to one tradition, he was slain by an Arab as he gazed upon the ruins he longed to see. At the moment of his death, it is said, he was singing his famous Ode to Zion, which contains this apostrophe to the promised land:

> Lo! It shall pass, shall change, the heritage
> Of vain-crowned kingdoms; not all time subdues
> Thy strength; thy crown endures from age to age.
> Thy God desired thee for a dwelling place;
> And happy is the man whom He shall choose,
> And draw him nigh to rest within thy space.[16]

Notes

1. All quotations from the text of the Talmud are taken from I. Epstein, ed. and trans., *The Babylonian Talmud*. References are to the folio page of the tractate cited.
2. The debt of the Talmudic Rabbis to Greek scientific vocabulary was demonstrated almost a century ago in Samuel Krauss, *Griechische und Lateinische Lehnworter im Talmud, Midrasch und Targum*.
3. Gerson Cohen, "Zion in Rabbinic Literature," in *Zion in Jewish Literature*, ed. Abraham S. Halkin (New York: Herzl Press, 1961), 71.
4. Chaim Dimitrovsky, "Zion in Medieval Literature," in *Zion in Jewish Literature*, 39.
5. Jehuda Halevi, *Selected Poems of Jehudah Halevi*, 157.
6. Jehuda Halevi, *The Kuzari (Kitab al Khazari): An Argument for the Faith of Israel*, 36.
7. Halevi, *Kuzari*, 44.
8. Halevi, *Kuzari*, 88.
9. Halevi, *Kuzari*, 88.
10. My translation from the Latin.
11. Talmudic views on the relation between climate and human health and intelligence, and the possible influence of Greco-Roman climatological doctrine on Jewish thinkers, are surveyed in detail in Stephen T. Newmyer, "The Concept of Climate and National Superiority in the Talmud and its Classical Parallels" and "Climate and Health: Classical and Talmudic Perspectives."
12. Halevi, *Kuzari*, 99.
13. Halevi, *Kuzari*, 242.
14. Halevi, *Kuzari*, 243.
15. On Galen's positive reception among Jewish physicians, one may note J. Snowman, *A Short History of Talmudic Medicine* 10, "The great influence of Galen on the medical science of his age was not exclusively due to the contributions which he made to medicine. Some of his

influence was due to the teleology which he infiltrated into his writings, by insisting that structure was exquisitely adapted to function, and by emphasizing the role of purpose and design in nature. This philosophy thus appealed to both the Jewish and Christian scholars who studied his writings, and later on these views of Galen coincided with the theological standpoint of the professors of Arabic medicine."

16. Halevi, *Selected Poems,* 155-56.

Works Cited

The Babylonian Talmud. Trans. and ed. I. Epstein. London: Soncino Press, 1935.

Cohen, Gerson. "Zion in Rabbinic Literature." *Zion in Jewish Literature.* Ed. Abraham S. Halkin. New York: Herzl Press, 1961. 38-64.

Dimitrovsky, Chaim. "Zion in Medieval Literature." *Zion in Jewish Literature.* Ed. Abraham S. Halkin. New York: Herzl Press, 1961. 65-82.

Halevi, Jehuda. *The Kuzari (Kitab al Khazari): An Argument for the Faith of Israel.* Trans. Hartwig Hirschfeld. New York: Schocken, 1971.

———. *Selected Poems of Jehudah Halevi.* Trans. Nina Salaman. Philadelphia: Jewish Publication Society of America, 1924.

Krauss, Samuel. *Griechische und Lateinische Lehnworter im Talmud, Midrasch und Targum.* Berlin: S. Calvary, 1899.

Newmyer, Stephen T. "The Concept of Climate and National Superiority in the Talmud and its Classical Parallels." *Transactions and Studies of the College of Physicians of Philadelphia* 5.5 (1983): 1-12.

———. "Climate and Health: Classical and Talmudic Perspectives." *Judaism* 33 (1984): 426-38.

Snowman, J. *A Short History of Talmudic Medicine.* London: John Bale, Sons and Danielsson, 1935.

# Astral and Tidal Phenomena, Earthquake Prediction, and the *Astronomical Clock* of Juan de Barrenechea

Robert J. Morris

Few periods are more important in the intellectual history of Hispanic America than the first two decades of the eighteenth century. A time in which the bonds of Scholasticism and the Baroque are just beginning to loosen their grip in Spanish America, these years also mark the beginning in the New World of the Enlightenment and of rational philosophies that were already dominant in Western Europe, particularly France. In Mexico, Lima, and other urban centers in Spanish-speaking America where scientists, artists, and free thinkers congregated, the universities now offered the most propitious environment for the promotion and dissemination of individual and collective contributions to the arts and the sciences.

While Sigüenza y Góngora in Mexico and Peralta de Barnuevo in Lima are generally considered epitomes of the best scholarship of the time, there are dozens of other New World scientists whose work, though less well known, is still considered just as significant as that of their contemporary luminaries. Juan Manuel de Barrenechea, a contemporary and compatriot of Peralta, is one of those who prospered intellectually in the environment of San Marcos University, yet never achieved a clearly defined academic or literary identity. Even though his scientific publications were known to the eighteenth-century community of academicians in Lima,[1] for instance, they did not afford him the national or international reputation enjoyed by Peralta.

The relative obscurity that has befallen Barrenechea in the intellectual annals of Peru is undoubtedly a result of historical and geographical coincidence with the foremost academician of the time in South America.

Barrenechea's principal work, his so-called *Astronomical Clock*, is not without value, however. It provides a significant, insightful view of the determination and rationale with which a representative academician of the early eighteenth-century in the New World sought to advance and substantiate his scientific hypotheses.

Neither the Spanish American histories of science nor those of literature have ever dealt clearly, or decisively, with Barrenechea's work. Only the title, *Relox Astrónomico* (with no critical commentary), is given by even the venerable nineteenth-century bibliographer, José Toribio Medina, in his *Biblioteca hispanoamericana* (213). In addition, since Barrenechea's death in 1729(?), the author's name has been confused with that of another of his contemporaries—Juan de Barrenechea y Albis, who died in 1707 and is generally known as the author of *La Restauración del Imperial y Conversión de los Infieles* (1693), a work in prose that some literary historians, such as Raimundo Lazo, cite in their discussion of the evolution of prose fiction in Spanish America (243-45). The confusion between Juan de Barrenechea and Juan de Barrenechea y Albis has originated in part from the fact that the latter, for most of his life a Mercedarian friar in Chile, is also associated with San Marcos. He spent a short time there studying theology. Thereafter the Chilean returned to Santiago, became embroiled with his bishop, and ultimately left again for Lima, where he published *La Restauración...* (known also as *La historia de Chile*). As it is easy to surmise, the true identities of the two Barrenecheas and of their publications also has been clouded because *La Restauracion...* has been credited to Juan de Barrenechea, author of *Relox Astronómico,* and not always to Juan de Barrenechea y Albis, the Chilean historian and friar.

During the latter years of Juan de Barrenechea, the recognition afforded his *Relox Astronómico* was clearly overshadowed by the frequency and popularity of the publications on astronomy by Peralta de Barnuevo. Even other facets of Barrenechea's academic and scientific achievements were the subject of inevitable comparisons with those of Peralta: the latter held the Cátedra de Matemáticas for which Juan de Barrenechea apparently was the substitute, Peralta's reputation as an astronomer was established even in France, and he was also the rector of the University of San Marcos. In addition to his writings on astronomy, Peralta authored texts on a wide variety of topics, from engineering studies to didactic drama and verse. Irving A. Leonard has noted Peralta's special fascination with and dedication to the study of the sun and moon:

> Las observaciones astronómicas eran, sin duda, para don Pedro su preocupación constante y predilecta.... Años después el Conde de Pontchartrian comunicó a la Academia Francesa de Ciencias las observaciones hechas por Peralta del eclipse de luna ocurrido en Diciembre de 1713, y fueron publicadas en la *Revista* de este instituto.

> Posteriormente se imprimieron en el mismo periódico las observaciones del peruano de otro eclipse de luna del 26 de marzo de 1717 y una obscuración total de ese satélite ocurrida el 27 de abril de 1725 . . . pruebas más convincentes de sus conocimientos astronómicos se encierran en su obra *Observaciones Astronómicas* (Lima, 1717) . . . . Desde 1709, y acaso antes, Peralta dio a luz anualmente una especie de lunario o almanaque con el título *El conocimiento de los tiempos,* en que indicaba la posición y los movimientos de los planetas y daba un calendario con datos de carácter geográfico e histórico. Hasta se atrevió a pronosticar terremotos, fenómenos naturales que turbaban con frecuencia la vida tranquila y apacible de la colonia. (12-13)

The circumstances that characterize the life of Peralta during the second decade of the eighteenth century clearly parallel those of Barrenechea and substantiate the intellectual and academic relationship these scholars shared. In addition to being "catedráticos" of the same subject matter in the same university, both were devoted to astronomy, at that time a natural complement to the study of mathematics. Moreover, Barrenechea and Peralta were specifically interested in the study of the sun, moon, and tides and their relationship with earthquakes. Indeed, Barrenechea's *Relox* . . . can be considered an important complement of Peralta's scientific attempts and publications meant to correlate known earthquakes in Europe and the Americas with predictable and measured relationships between the sun, the moon, and the tides.

The only extant copy of *Relox Astronómico* known to be in the United States is in the possession of Brown University. Moreover, it is a microfilm copy of the original text known to be in the Biblioteca Nacional de Chile in Santiago. The accompanying transcription of *Relox* . . . is based on the microfilm copy. The work consists of fourteen pages of text, including the title page and astronomical statistics which, according to the author, verify his discovery that earthquakes occur in the first twelve hours and twenty four minutes of the day or the lunar cycle:

> siempre que á temblado la Tierra . . . a sido en las doce horas y veinte y quatro minutos, que nuestro Relox Astronómico señala, y no en las otras doce horas y veinte y quatro minutos restantes del dia o circulo lunar.

Barrenechea also claims that his work reveals two other of nature's secrets. The first is that all natural deaths occur in the first half of the same day or lunar circle. The second is the coincidence of earthquakes and ebb tides with the first twelve hours and twenty-four minutes of the day or lunar cycle. As Barrenechea explains his findings:

> Y ensuma de lo tratado asta aqui se saca que en las 12. horas y 24 m. que nuestro Relox señala mengua el Mar, Espira la Criatura, y tiembla la Tierra, Y al contrario en las otras 12. horas, y 14 m. restantes del dia, o círculo Lunar crece el Mar, no espira la Criatura, ni tiembla la Tierra.

After the initial explanation of the above, Barrenechea includes a chart for predicting earthquakes in Lima in 1726, "Conjunción, oposición, Quartos Crecientes y Menguantes." This is followed by the perpetual and universal astronomical clock based on a thirty-day month with the hours of each day in which mankind will die naturally and the ebb tide will occur. The third major division of the text, "Explicación de la fábrica y uso de el Relox Astronómico," explains the use of the preceding tables, Barrenechea's abbreviations, and an explanation of the mathematical adjustments necessary in the perpetual and universal clock in order to make accurate predictions of earthquakes in the future. A final note warns that church clocks frequently do not give the correct time and that care should be exercised if one depends on such a clock to know the correct hour.

The remainder of the text, "Recopilación de los Terremotos," is divided into two sections, America and Europe. It is an accounting by years of the most memorable earthquakes and includes commentary on how they coincide with the tides and conjunctions of the sun and moon as predicted by the *Relox Astronómico*. For the Americas, the earliest recorded by Barrenechea is 1606, those of 1725 being the last entries. For Europe, 365 is the first year for which there is an entry, and 1703 is the last. There are 57 entries in all. Due to the limitations of space and to the length of "Recopilación...," only representative portions are included herein. Throughout the entire transcription, considerable effort has been made to assure that all accents (or the lack thereof) and spellings are faithful to the original text. In those cases of blurred or illegible text in the original (e.g. in the case of ink bled from one side of the page to the other), the assumed meaning has been rendered. Notice is given in the two instances in which words are missing from the last line or two of the microfilm.

Note

1. According to J.T. Medina, in *Biblioteca hispanoamericana 1493-1810* (213), a list of Barrenechea's writings and achievements is recorded in *"Relación de los méritos, títulos, y grados del Doctor Don Juan Manuel de Barrenechea, Colegial del Real y Mayor de San Phelipe de Lima, y Abogado de aquella Real Audiencia, natural de la Ciudad de los Reyes del Perú, y originario del Reyno de Navarra.* Fol.3, páginas sin foliar y final bl. 15 de Julio de 1729."

Works Consulted

Lazo, Raimundo. *Historia de la literatura hispanoamericana. El período colonial* (1492-1780). México: Editorial Porrúa, 1969.

Leonard, Irving A. *Obras dramáticas de Pedro Peralta de Barnuevo*, Santiago de Chile: Imprenta Universitaria, 1937.

Medina, José Toribio. *Biblioteca Hispano-Chilena, 1523-1817.* Tomo 1, Amsterdam: N. Israel, 1965.

——, *Biblioteca hispanoamericana 1493-1810.* Tomo cuarto, 1701-1767, Amsterdam: N. Israel, 1968.

Relox Astronomico De Temblores De La Tierra, Secreto Maravilloso De La Naturaleza, Descubierto, Y Hallado Por D. Juan De Barrenechea, substituto de la Cathedra de Prima de Mathematicas de esta Real Universidad de San Marcos de la Ciudad de Lima Ala Serenissima Emperatriz de los Cielos Madre de Dios, y Sa Nuestra De El Camino Que Con Reverendo Culto Se venera en el antiquisissimo y sumptuoso Templo de la Ciudad de Pamplona, Corte novilíssima del Esclarecido Reyno de Navarra Con licencia de los Superiores En Lima, en la Imprenta Antuerpiana, que esta en la Calle Real de Palacio. Año de 1725.

A MARIA SANTISIMA DE EL CAMINO

No podian Señora mis pobres estudiosas reflecciones solicitar para asilo otro numen, que el Vuestro; â cuyo mar debieron en gracia mis talentos lo que le recivieron de agua en el Baptismo. Alla se van aquellas, MADRE MIA DE EL CAMINO, sin que quieran ganar por voluntarias lo que perdieran a no confesarse a Vuestro Trono ciegamente precisas. No quiero blasonar de obsequio, lo que es innata inclinacion del alma, pues nada debe, ni al rapto de las plumas la Esphera, ni a la velocidad de los graves el centro, subiendo va esos Orves con arta invidia mia mi Relox Astronomico. No la tenga como el canta, a sus obras el Poeta mas humano quando á Roma caminan parve, *nec invideo, fineme; liber ibis in verbem,* que como eran obras de amar, y la mia es de amaros, no merece invidia el caminar amando, sellad pues ô Relox mio con vuestro labio humilde la huella de la mejor ara, que Navarra venera, y sobra la elevacion de ese pie, para que os miren con respecto las Nubes. Nube era la que tomó a su cargo la dilatada conducta del Hebreo, y ni en la noche tropezó a la sombra de su farol brillante el cansado Ysraelita, ni de dia le faltó director en su Columna, por que sabe la milagrosa Nube del CAMINO, que celebra Pamplona, mudar colores para variar los Beneficios, el prodigio es, que especulando Elias desde la Cathedra de su elevado carmelo este aspecto venefico, observó ser como la huella, o pisada de un hombre *quasi vestigium hominis* porque, como era aquel hermoso milagroso signo la Señora, a quien ofrece culto el caminante, precisamente se avia de dar à conocer como vestigio. A la sombra de esta celestial pisada encamina la sombra de mi Relox lineas, para que si como Nube en el Mar me encaminô libre de escollos ala America, como ya à subido à la Region Etherea *ascendebat de mari* desaga los aspectos malevolos detếblores de la Tierra, y pues â Vuestro magisterio o Relox Soberano, debe mi Astronomico el probable conocimiếto de sus horas, y tiempos, no ceseis de patrocinarme como siempre, y ostếte vuestro poder su mayor maravilla en transformarme en no tan

    indignisimo esclavo de Vuestra Mag;
    postrado a Vuestros Soberanos pies
    Don Juan de Barrenechea

    La predicion del dia, y hora que a de temblar la tierra es dificultosísima, por quanto concurren para este efecto, dos causas principales â un mismo tiempo, cuya conbinacion es impenetrable al scrutinio humano. La una es aquella materia o copia de Exalaciones que se forma en lo mas concavo de la segunda Region de la tierra, cuya parte convexa dista siete estados de nuestros pies; la otra es el influjo de los planetas, que estos con sus aspectos, assi como remueven los Elementos y causan las tempestades conmueven tambien la materia de que se preceden los temblores.

    Y de cerca de esto, investigando con estudioso desbelo, y fatiga, por los efectos las causas, el secreto maravilloso, que por repetidas observaciones proprias é descuvierto, y hallado es, que siempre, que á temblado la Tierra en Lima, y en otras partes, a sido en las doce horas, y veinte y quatro minutos, que nuestro Relox Astronomico señala, y no en las otras doce horas y veinte y quatro minutos restantes del dia o circulo Lunar, como se reconoce de las observaciones de los Temblores grandes y pequeños que se anotaran al fin de esta Obra: Y si los Temblores que ubiere en el año de 1726 convinieren con las horas que nuestro Relox Astronomico señala, juzgo prudente lector se abra conseguido la calificacion y certidumbre del mas admirable secreto de la naturaleza; en tantos siglos ignorado, y con el, un beneficio universal para los Reynos, y Provincias de Europa, Asia, Africa y America, que padecen el espantoso subsidio de Temblores por la quietud y sosiego con que se podra bibir en aquellas doze horas, y viente y quatro minutos, que no tiembla la Tierra; de lo qual tendre singular complacencia por los mucho q̃ deseo servir a la Republica con mas viles obsequios, y ala ingeniosissima y docta Astronomia lustre, y esplendor de la novilissima ciencia de las Mathematicas, cõ otros nuevos Problemas, q̃ mas la exalten, y aplaudã.

    Y por q̃ se de mas acenso, a este prodigioso secreto bemos otros dos, no menos admirables, que se experimentã, desde la antiguedad en las mismas doze horas, y veinte y quatro minutos, que nuestro Relox Astronomico señala. El uno es, que toda criatura, que muere de muerte natural espira, y acava el ultimo aliento de la vida, en estas doze horas, y veinte y quatro minutos, y nunca en las otras doze horas y veinte y quatro minutos restantes del dia o circulo Lunar, como lo refieren Aristoteles, Plinio, Pedro Aponiense y otros muchos; y por esta causa es tambien util, y muy necesario nuestro Relox para los Medicos Espirituales, que aiudan a bien morir a los enfermos. El otro secreto, que tanto admiran los hombres es, el continuo flujo, y reflujo del mar con igual orden de 6. horas, y 12 m. en cada uno y siempre, que se hace el de las dos menguantes es, en las 12 horas, y 24. m. que nuestro Relox señala; y segun nuestras observaciones, (caso raro) parece, que el temblor aguarda, q̃ el mar se retire de sus margenes, ó playas abriendole el camino, que ocupa con sus aguas en las entrañas de la primera Region de la Tierra, para salir à hacer su efecto, acia nosotros, con furioso, y espantoso estruendos, vemos, tambien, en algunos Terremotos grandes, que a avido el extraordinario efecto de averse retirado el Mar una legua, y mas, de donde se colige la especial conexion, que tienen los Temblores de la Tierra, con las crecientes, y menguantes del Mar, pues como se manifiesta en nuestras observaciones, solo tiembla la tierra durante la menguante del Mar, y no en las otras 12. horas, y 24 m. de la creciente: Y ensuma de lo tratado asta aqui se saca que en las 12. horas y 24 m. que nuestro Relox señala mengua el Mar, Espira la Criatura, y tiembla la Tierra, Y al contrario en las otras 12. horas, y 14 m. restantes del dia, o circulo Lunar crece el Mar, no espira la Criatura, ni tiembla la Tierra.

Tal vez á acontecido, y acontecerá, que despues de un gran terremoto, tiemble la Tierra a todas horas, en las 24. de uno, o mas dias, y entonces precisamente alugnos de estos Temblores, que repiten (que siempre suelen ser pequeños) acaeceran, no solo en las 12. horas, que nuestro Relox señala, sino tambien en las otras 12 horas, y 24 m. restantes del dia, o circulo Lunar; sin que por eso sea incierto nuestro maravilloso secreto, y observaciones; Por quanto un gran Terremoto de estos, que antecede (el qual ya vemos en nuestras observaciones, que siempre a acaecido en las horas que nuestro Relox señala) es un extremo irregular de la naturaleza, que con aquel gran movimiento, que à causado en la Tierra, abre algunas concavidades, (retirandose el Mar con extraordinaria distancia como ya se dijo) y asta q̃ con repetidos fluxos, y refluxos se cierran a aquellas concavidades, o agujeros, está freqüetemente saliendo por ellos, la materia de q̃ se procede el Temblor. Y juzgo que si se hiciere observacion en tales acaecimientos, q̃ la mayor parte de los Temblores pequeños, que repiten, despues del grande, q̃ antecede, acaeceran naturalmente en las horas que nro. Relox señala, y pocos en las otras 12. horas restantes del dia, ó circulo Lunar, y para esto, es eficaz convencimiento lo q̃ dice el Historiador Antonio de Herrera en la Decada V. Lib. X. pag. 293. aũ sin aver tenido luz de nuestro secreto, y observaciones, y dice assi; La causa por q̃ las tierras maritimas son sugetas á temblores, parece q̃ procede de tener el agua tapados los agujeros, y averturas de la tierra por donde avia de despedir las exalaciones calientes, q̃ se engendran en ella, y la humedad condesada de la superficie de la tierra con la sequedad, q̃ por defuera causan el Sol, y vientos hacen que se encierren mas adentro los vapores calientes, q̃ encendidos vienen a romper. Vale.

Conjunciones y Oposiciones, Quartos Crecientes, y Menguantes de Sol, y Luna, ajustados puntualissimamente al Meridiano de Lima para el Año de 1726, que serviran para la observacion de los temblores, que en el acaecieren.

	D.H.M.			D.H.M.	
ENERO			**JULIO**		
Conj.	3. 7.35.	del dia	Q. crec.	6. 3.56.	delamañ
Qua.cre.	11. 5.33.	delamañ	Oposi.	14. 2.15.	delamañ
Oposi.	17. 7.40.	delanoc	Q.mēg.	22. 2.59.	delamañ
Q.mēg.	24.10.31.	delanoc.	Conj.	28. 7.10.	delanoc.
FEBRERO			**AGOSTO**		
Conj.	2. 2.08.	delamañ	Q.crec.	4. 2.41.	delatard.
Qua.cre.	9. 4.51.	delatard.	Oposi.	12. 5.26.	delatard.
Oposi.	16. 8.26.	deldia	Q.mēg.	20. 2.25.	delatard.
Q.mēg.	23. 4.37.	delatard.	Conj.	27. 2.35.	delamañ
MARZO			**SEPTIEMBRE**		
Conj.	3. 7.03.	delanoc.	Q.crec.	3. 7.12.	deldia
Qua.cre.	11. 1.22.	delamañ	Oposi.	11. 8. 8.	deldia
Oposi.	17. 7.54.	delanoc.	Q.mēg.	18. 7.31.	delanoc.
Q.mēg.	25.12.14.	deldia Eclipse	Conj.	25. 1.47.	deldia
ABRIL			**OCTUBRE**		
Conj.	2. 9.28.	deldia	Q.crec.	2.10.29.	denoc.
Qua.cre.	9. 7.51.	deldia Eclipse	Oposi.	10.11.37.	denoc.
Oposi.	16. 8.15.	deldia	Q.mēg.	18. 2. 5.	delamañ
Q.mēg.	24. 7.11.	deldia	Conj.	24.11.21.	denoc.
MAYO			**NOVIEMBRE**		
Conj.	1. 9.15.	delanoc.	Q.crec.	1. 1. 5.	delatar.
Qua.cre.	8. 1.37.	delatard.	Oposi.	9. 1.36.	delatar.
Oposi.	15. 9.42.	delanoc.	Q.mēg.	16. 9.40.	deldia
Q.mēg.	22. 0.06.	delamañ	Conj.	23. 1.55.	delatar.
Conj	31. 5.27.	delamañ			
JUNIO			**DICIEMBRE**		
Qua.cre.	6. 7.05.	delamañ	Q.crec.	1. 3.21.	delatar.
Oposi.	14.10.54.	deldia	Oposic.	9. 1.50.	delam.
Q.mēg.	22. 2.53.	delatard.	Q.mēg.	15. 6.36.	delatar.
Conj.	29.12.44.	deldia	Conj.	23. 6.48.	delam.
			Q.crec.	31.11.42.	deldia.

Y por que, en qualquiera de estos Aspectos allandose la Luna en el Ascendente suele causar los [last word or so cut off]

Relox Astronomico
Perpetuo y Universal

Circular drawing to left of the following: Que aun mismo tiempo nos señala la tierra, que espira la criatura, q̃ muere de muerto natural, y que mengua el Mar.

In the left margin, to the left of "Dias," is a moon figure and then "EDAD DE LA LUNA" written vertically.

Dias	H.M.	H.M.	H.M.	H.M.
1 delas	2. 48. M. àlas	9. 00. D y delas	3. 12. T. àlas	9. 24. M.
2 de	3. 36. m. à	9. 48. d y de	4. 00. t. à	10. 12. n.
3 de	4. 24. m. à	10. 36. d. y de	4. 48. t. à	11. 00. n.
4 de	5. 12. m. à	11. 24. d. y de	5. 36. t. à	11. 48. n.
5 de	6. 00. m. à	12. 12. d. y de	6. 24. t. à	12. 36. n.
6 de	6. 48. m. à	1. 00. t. y de	7. 12. n. à	1. 24. ds.
7 de	7. 36. m. à	1. 48. t. y de	8. 00. n. à	2. 12. ds.
8 de	8. 24. D. à	2. 36. t. y de	8. 48. n. à	3. 00. ds.
9 de	9. 12. D. à	3. 24. t. y de	9. 36. n. à	3. 48. ds.
10 de	10. 00. D. à	4. 12. t. y de	10. 24. n. à	4. 36. ds.
11 de	10. 48. D. à	5. 00. T. y de	11. 12. n. á	5. 24. ds.
12 de	11. 36. D. á	5. 48. T. y de	12. 00. n. à	6. 12. ds
13 de	0. 48. m. à	7. 00. D. y de	1. 12. t. á	7. 24. N.
14 de	14. 36. m. â	7. 48. D. y de	2. 00. t. à	8. 12. N.
15 de	2. 24. m. à	8. 36. D. y de	2. 48. t. à	9. 00. N.
16 de	3. 12. m. á	9. 24. D. y de	3. 36. t. à	9. 48. N.
17 de	4. 00. m. á	10. 12. D. y de	4. 24. t. â	10. 36. N.
18 de	4. 48. m. à	11. 00. D. y de	5. 12. t. â	11. 24. N.
19 de	5. 36. m. à	11. 48. D. y de	6. 00. t. â	12. 12. n.
20 de	6. 24. m. á	12. 36. D. y de	6. 48. t. à	1. 00. ds.
21 de	7. 12. m. à	1. 24. T. y de	7. 36. N. à	1. 48. ds.
22 de	8. 00. D. à	2. 12. T. y de	8. 24. N. á	2. 36. ds.
23 de	8. 48. D. à	3. 00. T. y de	9. 12. N. à	3. 24. ds.
24 de	9. 36. D. à	3. 48. T. y de	10. 00. N. à	4. 12. ds.
25 de	10. 24. D. à	4. 36. T. y de	10. 48. N. à	5. 00. ds.
26 de	11. 12. D. à	5. 24. D. y de	11. 36. N. à	5. 48. ds.
27 de	12. 00. D. à	6. 12. D. y de	12. 24. N. à	6. 36. ds.
28 de	1. 12. M. à	7. 24. D. y de	1. 36. T. à	7. 48. N.
29 de	2. 00. M. à	8. 12. D. y de	2. 24. T. à	8. 36. N.
30 de	2. 48. M. à	9. 00. D. y de	2. 12. T. à	9. 24. N.

Explicacion De La Fabrica Y Uso De El Reloj Astronomico

La Raiz y principio de la fabrica de este Relox Astronomico es, el instante en que llega la Luna cada dia à aquel milagroso meridiano ABC, que divide en dos iguales partes el quadrante oriental de qualquiera Emispherio.

Lo que unicamente hemos de saber para el uso de este Relox es el dia de la Conjuncion de Sol, y Luna; y si la Conjuncion fuere á las 9. de la manana, y la Oposicion a las 9. de la noche, será en toda aquella Lunacion puntual, y fixo nuestro Relox, sin que sea necessario añadir, ni quitar cosa alguna à las horas que señala.

EXEMPLO. Quiero saber el dia 24. de Enero de 1726. las horas que tiembla la tierra; veo en la Tabla de las Conjunciones, que la antecedente al temblor serâ el dia 3. de dicho Mes, y suponiendo, que esta Conjuncion fuesse á las nueve de la mañana, y la Oposicion (que es à 1.7 de dicho Mes) a las nueve de la noche; contarè la edad que tenia la Luna y hallo que desde el dia 3. que fue la Conjuncion, hasta el dia propuesto 24. de Enero han corrido 22. dias incluso el de la Conjuncion, que assi se han de contar, y el Relox Astronomico â los 22. dias de la edad de la Luna me señala, que si temblare la tierra, será desde las 8. horas de la mañana, hasta las 2. horas, y 12. minutos de la tarde, y desde las 8. horas y 24. minutos de la noche hasta las 2. horas y 26. minutos del dia siguiente.

Pero si la Conjuncion precedente al temblor fuere antes ó despues de las nueve de la mañana, ó la Oposicion precedente al temblor, antes, ô despues de la nueve de la noche, he de añadir, ò quitar à las horas, que nuestro Relox señala, dos minutos por cada hora, que son los que con poca diferencia camina la Luna con el movimiento natural de su Orve, ò deferente eccentrico en una hora; como v.g. si la Conjuncion de Sol, y Luna es, la que precede al dia que quiero saber las horas, que tiembla la tierra, y esta Conjuncion fuere 6. horas antes de las 9. de la mañana, he de añadir 12. minutos á las horas que nuestro Relox señala, por quanto estos 12. minutos despues de las 9. de la mañana, llegaria la Luna el dia de esta Conjuncion al prodigioso meridiano, que divide en dos iguales partes el quadrante oriental de nuestro Emispherio, y si la Conjuncion fuere seis horas despues de las 9. de la mañana, quitare 12. minutos de las horas que nuestro Relox señala. Si la Oposicion de Sol, y Luna es la que precede al dia que quiero saber las horas que tiembla la tierra, y esta Oposicion fuere, supongo tambien 6. horas antes de las 9. de la noche, he de añadir 12. minutos á las horas que nuestro Relox señala, y si fuere la Oposicion seis horas despues, he de quitar 12 minutos, que son 2 minutos por cada hora como ha se dijo y de este modo se abra arreglado nuestro Relox tanto que la diferencia sea insensible en toda aquella Lunacion. Las abreviaciones del

Relox son estas con la letra D. Se denotan las horas del dia, con la N. la noche, con la T. la tarde, con la M. la mañana, y con la Ds. las horas del dia siguiente, y estas horas se cuentan como la Iglesia cuenta de media noche â media noche.

En los Reloxes de las Iglesias suele haver algunas vezes mucha desigualdad y especialmente en tiempo de Invierno, que muchos dias seguidos en este Emispherio, suele no verse el Sol con el qual se arreglan los Reloxes de campana. Tambien el temblor puede tener su principio en otro Meridiano mui distante de nosotros, y dilatarse algun tiempo en llegar, y si tal vez huviere diferencia de minutos, en las observaciones de los temblores, que de oy en adelante acaecieren en Lima, puede ser por alguna de estas dos causas, y no por defecto de nuestro Relox Astronomico.

Recopilacion De Los Terremotos

mas memorables, que à avido en esta America Austral, y en Europa, y de sus observaciones consta, que todos sucedieron en las doze horas y veinte y quatro minutos, que nuestro Relox Astronomico señala.

AMERICA

Año de 1606

Dia Jueves Santo 23 de Marzo, a las 3 dadas dela tarde se estremeciò furiosamente la tierra en la Ciudad de Sãa, y muriò á esta misma hora en aquella Ciudad, Sãto Thoribio Arcobispo de Lima, como lo refiere D. Francisco de Echave, en su tratado de la Estrella de Lima convertida en Sol: fue la precedente Conjuncion al suceso, dia 8 de Marzo à las 3 horas y 6 minutos de la tarde del Relox de Sãta, y la edad de la Luna 16 dias incluso el dia de la Conjuncion, y por que esta fue 6 horas despues de las 9 horas de la mañana, se han de quitar 12 minutos de las horas que nuestro Relox señala, como ya se à advertido en la explicacion del uso del Relox, y concuerda con el, esta observacion.

Año de 1618

Dia de San Balentin 14 de Febrero, entre seis y siete de la mañana huvo en la Ciudad de Truxillo un gran terremoto, y se vio en el Ciclo una Columna de fuego, a modo de Cometa, que se desapareciò luego, y el Señor Obispo y su Secretario muriero de espanto, referelo el sapientissimo Juan Zahn Canonigo reglar Premonstratense, en su Historia Mathematica fue la Conjuncion precedente al conflicto, el dia 20 de Enero á las cinco y media de la mañana del Relox de Truxillo, y la edad de la Luna veinte dias, y conviene esta observacion con las horas, que nuestro Relox Astronomico señala.

Año de 1724

Dia 4 de Septiembre á las 8 horas y tres quartos de la mañana huvo otro temblor que remeció dos veces, con mucha fuerza, y la Conjuncion fue á 18 de Agosto horas 4 y minutos 20 de la mañana, y la edad de la Luna 18 dias: luego corresponde á nuestro Relox Astronomico.

Año de 1725

Dia Martes Santo, 27 de Marzo, como á las 8 de la mañana huvo en la Ciudad de Santiago de Chile, un gran temblor, fue la Conjuncion antes de este espantoso acaecimiento à 14 de dicho mes, á las 8 horas de la mañana, y la edad de la Luna 14 dias: luego corresponde.

Año de 1725

Dia de Pascua de Reyes, 6 de Enero, a las once y media del dia, huvo en Lima un temblor grande, que duró dos credos, fue la Conjuncion precedente á 15 de Diciembre 1724 á las doce del dia, y teniendo la Luna 23 dias, conviene ampliamente esta observacion cō nuestro Relox.

EUROPA

Año de 365

Dia 20 de Agosto al amanecer, tembló furiosamente la Tierra en todo el Ymperio Romano, y aviendo sido la Conjuncion el dia 9. tenia la Luna 12 dias de edad incluso el de la Conjuncion, y conviene esta observacion ampliamente con nuestro Relox, y este temblor y los siguientes son del Doctisimo Juan Zahn ya citado.

Año de 1200

Dia 3 de Mayo á hora de medio dia, huvo en el Reyno de Polonia un grā terremoto, fue la Conjunciō antes a 23 de Abril, y teniendo la Luna 11 dias, corresponde esta observacion à nuestro Relox.

Año de 1694

Dia 8 de Septiembre à las 12 del dia, cuenta el mismo R.P. Privitera, que huvo en Napoles un gran terremoto, que causò mucha ruina en el Principado de la Basilicata, y en otras partes de la Costa, fuè la Conjunciō à 20 de Agosto horas 8 de la noche, del Relox de Napoles, y tenia la Luna 20 dias, y en ellos nro. Relox señala, q̃ si tēblare la tierra, serà desde las 6 horas, y 24 minutos de la mañana, asta las 12 horas, y 36 minutos del dia; Luego cōviene esta observacion.

Año de 1703

Dia Domingo 14 de Enero, huvo en Aguila Ciudad de Ytalia à las 2 horas dela noche, q̃ à nro. Relox de España correspõde à las 8 de la noche un horrẽdo terremoto, q̃ maltratò muchos Edificios, como se refiere en una relacion de los milagros de S. Phelipe Neri, que imprimierõ en Lima los V. Padres del Oratorio fue la Conjuncion à 18 de Diciẽbre de 1702 y teniẽdo la Luna 28 incluso de la Conjuncion. Corresponde este acaecimiento, a nro. Relox Astronomico.

Que las horas de 57 temblores, que asta aqui emos referido y observado, que son todos los que con dia y hora fija se an podido adquirir desde el año de 365 de nuestra Redempcion ayan convendio con las horas, que nuestro Relox Astronomico señala, no parece mera casualidad, si una especial virtud, que para este efecto les dio el Autor de la naturaleza a los Aspectos Sol lunares, con la llegada de la Luna a los quatro prodigiosos meridianos que dividen en parte iguales los quatro quadrantes de la Esphera recta de qualquiera Emispherio; y ultimamente para que nuestro maravilloso secreto tenga en la posterioridad la estimacion, que mereciere, observaremos los temblores, que de oy en adelante huviere y se dará a su tiempo noticia de ellos. Y si Dios nuestro Señor es servido. se descubran y allen no solo este si no tambien otros mas prodigiosos secretos de viles instrumentos bastan.

DEUS SUPER OMNIA

 Zola's Uses of Climate in *The Land*

Wendell McClendon

Emile Zola's novels are always grounded in realistic detail. A cursory glance over the preparatory materials of any one novel is convincing; there are notes taken from books and from interviews, newspaper clippings, personal letters, etc., all designed to fill in the gaps in the novelist's knowledge and understanding of his subject.[1] Zola's writings are also grounded in the naturalistic theory which he outlined in *The Experimental Novel* (*Le Roman expérimental*) of 1880. His plan had been announced in 1870, in the subtitle to the *Rougon-Macquart* series: this was to be the "Natural and Social History of a Family Under the Second Empire."[2] More precisely, the naturalist wanted to discover the effects upon certain temperaments of a given historical moment and milieu. Yet, Zola scholars such as Guy Robert have demonstrated again and again that the author often ignored or distorted his sources,[3] and that as a consequence, the realism and the theory of natural determination, and even the plan to create a novel cycle to end all cycles, took back seats to other considerations. These other considerations are in my view artistic. I propose to demonstrate, via a close reading of *The Land* (*La Terre*), one of Zola's most naturalistic works, that uses of climate, the principal element of realistic detail of the physical milieu in the novel, are finally more artistic than mimetic, and that this artistic rendering of reality ultimately both informs and affirms the naturalist's agenda and its outcomes.[4]

The novelist's uses of the imagery of climate fit into a very long tradition. The seasonal cycle in particular—the most frequent manifestation of climate imagery—occurs often in ancient texts. Connections between the seasons and the four *elements*—earth, air, fire, and water—supposedly represented, even into the pre-modern era, a scientific view of nature and reflected universal harmony in the cosmos; but by the sixteenth century, the connections, the elements, and the seasons became mostly convenient clichés and ordering or intensifying techniques (Jareño 421-24). The revival of seasonal imagery in sixteenth-century France led to the rediscovery of the theory of climates, which eighteenth-century thinkers such as l'abbé Dubos, Buffon, and Montesquieu rejuvenated to support French nationalism (Fink 10; Sklar 319-22). Their geographical biases proved less interesting to later writers, however, than the very cyclical nature of seasonal movement, which suggests at least an ordered reading (Kuizinga 385) and at most an optimistic view of life, usually positing winter as the terminal season and thus as both a season of death and a time of acceptance and reconciliation.[5]

The clichés, the intensification, the elements even, and especially the orderliness of seasonal imagery remain active in the modern period, in France and elsewhere.[6] Zola was clearly aware of all of them: the tendency to connect youth and beauty to spring, passion and violence to summer, dissolution to autumn, and death to winter, are evident in his works; and the connections with earth-air-fire-water, although modified, are not altogether absent. However, there are a number of significant differences between Zola's uses of the seasons and those of other writers, past and present.

The naturalist was not at all interested in using any aspect of *The Land*, climatic or otherwise, to promote French nationalism.[7] He just as certainly chose the Beauce as his setting with clear purpose. As Henry James once put it, Zola "confounded" the human and the non-human "with the air and the weather, the rain and the shine, in the play of the elements themselves" (Tintner 97). The generally temperate Beauce, with its distinct seasonal variations,[8] offered the variety of conditions which corresponded to the notion of nature, human and otherwise, that he wished to "confound" in his story about agriculture. Going round and round in never-ending circles, nature's seasons offered hope to those who lived on the land, then delivered them despair, modeling the movements of the hearts, minds, and bodies of humans, who followed the seasons from joy to passion to wisdom to death, but who, unlike nature, were not able to survive what became for them a most vicious circle.

Moreover, a small town in a wheat-growing region, inhabited by ill-educated, poor peasants dominated by a few wealthy locals, by outside political and economic forces beyond their ken, and by their own brutish natures, provided the perfect frame for a tale of bread, which sustains life, and of blood, which both generates life and ensures its destruction. The peasants might struggle all they liked to rise in their world, they were finally pitted only against each other, by those more clever than they, as well as against the natural environment, and they ended, at best, in blind acceptance and resignation, supported neither by a felt spiritual life nor, especially, by the certainty that their blood somehow mattered. Their own children were most eager to dispossess and even to dispatch already burdensome parents so that the new generation might harvest the ever-diminishing fruits of ever-smaller parcels of land—until this *new* generation, in its turn, became the *old* generation, and so on and on. Zola visited the setting for *The Land* prior to beginning composition. He already knew country scenes and sights very well, since he had grown up wandering the fields and meadows near Aix. Consequently, none of his readers has faulted the realism of his version of geographical and weather conditions in the Beauce. His invented village also escapes reproach, even if the language and attitudes of his peasants do not.[9] In addition, Zola was on solid scientific ground in subjecting the temperaments of his characters to climatic effects. Donald Sutherland's 1987 article is only one of many arguing the impact of bad weather and thus of poor crops on the makers of the French Revolution.[10] Still, none of these factual matters weighs heaviest, for while the climate of Zola's Beauce is founded in matters of fact, it is realized in invented conditions and events and in their impact upon plants, animals, and people. Clearly more than climate actually experienced or even strictly conceived, it is indeed finally the whole physical milieu of the fictional village of Rognes and the surrounding Beauce countryside—earth, air, sky, sun, moon, clouds, rain, plants, people, and the very buildings, as they move through time and space—and in the end, the principal focus is on the novelist's success in ordering interactions between the elements, the land, the characters and the events, to guide the reader toward certain conclusions.

The first conclusion to be drawn from studying the climate of this novel is recognition that for Zola the climate, the physical milieu, far from being simply a sign of individual or social characteristics, exists both apart from and partially dependent upon the social milieu. Second, climate serves initially as a backdrop for the actions arising out of social intercourse, and then as an image of, or a reason for, or perhaps even a cause of those actions. Third, as climatic conditions and events move through evident seasonal cycles, they apparently become increasingly independent of the social milieu, and as they come to occupy the foreground, clearly limited human affairs fade to background. And lastly, climate thus foregrounded contributes to a model for eternal life which does not privilege human beings and which thereby exposes and imposes what David Baguley has called "the ultimate scandal of naturalist fiction: life is its own negation" (223).

This final outcome of *The Land*, the emergence of climate as a major character, depends upon all phases and aspects of the presentation of climate, so let us return to the first phase, at the beginning of the novel. The story opens on a late-October day in 1859 or so (367-68), when France is just feeling the effects of an agricultural crisis caused by over-production and foreign competition.[11] The weather is cool, gray, damp; the fields are green and red with rye and alfalfa; where the bare, yellow soil is exposed, golden wheat seeds fall in clouds from sowers' hands into the waiting furrows.

Jean Macquart, an ex-soldier who has only recently taken up the rural life, moves back and forth planting wheat. His is the individual point of view that will dominate human affairs from beginning to end. At this point in the story, the approaching cold, the soot-colored sky, the dull, unchanging light, all of these have little or no effect on Jean. Indeed, as the reader moves through Part I, the gap between the described physical milieu and Jean's mood slowly widens. After ten pages, the climate has practically taken on a separate existence. North toward Chartres, the capital city of the Beauce, the horizon is a thin black line joining the sky above and the land below in "a brownish, earthy unity." Against this setting, the sowers seem so many insects, "busy as black ants" swarming across the land (377).

Near the end of the first part, though, a kind of reversal occurs. Winter has arrived; the month is now November, and the intense cold and the snow drive people and animals inside (420-21). As Jean steps out onto the snow and looks up at the night sky, the heavens suddenly turn bright and clear. Stars are everywhere; one star shoots across the sky. Thoughts of Bethlehem's star are unavoidable, and such thoughts are reinforced by Jean's apparent feelings about the now-planted land. The whitened mounds of earth rising and falling away to the horizon seem the pregnant body of a woman, spread over with ermine covers, warm and secure, waiting for the spring sun to wake her (438). Jean has been transformed from one of many busy ants, and even from the simple, idealistic outsider of the opening pages, into the image of the contented, perhaps blessed, husband, watching his pregnant wife sleep and feeling pleased with himself and with the future of the human race.

This transparent anthropomorphism reveals at least part of what Zola meant when he said, "The earth is the heroine of my book" (ms. fol. 400). The land has in fact become a kind of independent character, sharing the scene with the chief human protagonist. If the latter, Jean, thinks at this point that the land is his to control, he has much to learn about life on the land, for the sun, not he, will play Prince Charming to his beauty and wake her in the spring, and Jean will have been only the soldier ant, servant to the Queen. The serene beauty of the winter climate, in short, foreshadows the essential independence of the physical milieu, which awaits not human actions to bring it to fruition, but the simple turning of the globe.

Here is early evidence of Zola's difference from the tradition. The story began in the fall, but it slips quickly and almost imperceptibly into the winter. At this point, the season fits the tradition, radiating hope for the future. This circumstance, like the slippage from fall to winter, is essentially deceptive though, since winter will prove anything but hopeful. Subsequent chapters and parts confirm the independence of the physical milieu, the uncertainty of the seasons, and the falseness of first impressions. The novelist takes the reader through the other seasons in turn, from the fall-winter of Part I to the spring-summer-fall of Parts II, III and IV, and back to the winter-spring of Part V. The clearly ordered movement spans some ten years and is not meant to represent historical seasons in the period 1859-1869, but rather typical seasons as defined by naturalists. In fact, all of the seasons are quite subject to ambivalence. The winter of Part I presents a late-fall to early-winter scenario; the reader is never sure, indeed, that winter has officially arrived. The uncertainty culminates in the winter of Part V, which begins in September and ends in March, when lingering winter is changing to spring. The vagueness is another way for Zola to remind the reader that the true issue of *The Land* is not human endeavors, conflicts, triumphs, failures, but the land itself, the physical milieu, the climate in fine—which is truly what dominates human existence: not some mysterious, disembodied fate but the very real, physical nature of nature, human and otherwise, in all of its uncertainties, whose product is not just bread for people but Life itself.

In the springtime of Part II, physical matters turn from their positive, affirming role toward the clearly negative. First, a blood vessel breaks in the brain of Mouche Fouan (454), the father of Jean's future wife, Françoise, and she and her sister Lise can only make futile gestures, such as rubbing his temples with cognac. Then, as the old man dies, a storm breaks, raining hailstones like musket shot, lighting the night sky with bluish flashes, and laying waste to crops and countryside, which resembles afterwards a body full of bullet wounds oozing life's blood. Everyone, including the two daughters, rushes out to view the damage (459-62).

These events, the stroke of Mouche Fouan and the storm, are recognizable as types of random occurrences which human beings often attribute to fate, in one form or another. Their coming together is at this point less evidence of a pathetic correspondence between human affairs and climatic disturbances than a sign that physical disaster can come from within and from without the human frame. Part II is in fact given over mostly to establishing for the novel the good and the evil that people do, in sexual, social, and political contexts. The physical climate thus plays a minor part, after the storm of Chapter II-2, as the story alternates between sexual duplicity, jealousy, burgeoning love, rising passions, greed, politics, commercial deception, and marriage. The grotesque marriage celebration of Chapter II-7 seems to set the seal on a pattern of increasing human degradation; the pattern continues and intensifies in Part III, as goodness virtually disappears from human interactions, and as the climate returns to a central role and joins forces, as it were, not with the best but with the worst of human impulses.

Part III is the summer scene, occurring some two years after the marriage of Lise to her cousin and Jean's friend, Buteau Fouan. Buteau had a child by Lise two years before marrying her. He married her only to get her land. He refused to accept his part of the paternal inheritance, because it was not the best of his father's land—until he could join it with his new wife's land. He cheated regularly at the marketplace, as he now cheats his father, Old Fouan, of the money due for the inheritance. And he is making every effort to seduce his wife's sister, Françoise, to make her his concubine in order to keep her land in his family.

This is the man upon whom, in Chapter III-1, the spring-summer climate of the Beauce smiles (531-35). With his shining-silver plow, Buteau dreams of "penetrating" the land, then "filling her belly full" with his seed. The earth in turn displays for him all her greenery. On fine mornings the rising sun clears the air of a pink fog to reveal the shimmering gold of wheat and the blues and purples of oats and rye; the surrounding buildings look like bright ships with great white sails on tall masts. The bad weather even avoids Buteau's land and destroys his neighbors' crops. The falling rain after a drought is for Buteau confirmation that God works for him.

The peasants of Rognes have little use for the deity, so the reader suspects at once that Buteau really refers to nature, to the physical milieu, to the climate, when he names God. It also appears that Buteau is right; natural, climatic conditions and events are thus no longer merely the results of some undefinable fate, now in favorable conjunction with human affairs, now not; they are rather collaborators in the plans of an ill-intentioned deity, the power behind material things, which brings violence and death to the land.

The middle of Part III takes violence to a climax. In Chapter III-4, as the peasants harvest wheat under a blazing August sun, Buteau tries once again to rape Françoise, to put his mark on the sixteen-year-old so that no other man may have her. She runs away—only to fall into the arms of Jean, who, though he loves her, cannot resist the temptation. In numb surprise, she is barely able to beg him to ejaculate on the ground (564-70). Almost at once, they hear the agonizing screams of a woman dying from heatstroke, forced to overwork by Buteau's greed. Death thus puts its mark upon the climate of violence and upon those who create it.

Death here is no longer the innocent, fateful stroke of Mouche Fouan, as in Chapter II-2, but neither is it yet the murderous death of Part V. Similarly, the climate in which the death occurs has, to some degree, excited the violence and caused the death, but the fullness of the climate's role is still not clear. Part IV and the first two chapters of Part V affirm Buteau's special relationship with the physical milieu, as they also generalize the human degradation first established in Part II. Climatic references are few, once again, but the intense personal and political struggles grow out of and reflect the climate, physical and social, which dominated Part III. Jean's marriage to Françoise causes turmoil ending in violence. The Emperor decides to back a different prefectoral candidate, one whose policies coincide with his own changed ones, and local politicians line up against their old political friend—and their own best interests—out of greed and blind loyalty to the Empire. Old Fouan becomes a tragic figure almost, as all his children cheat him of his due and even turn him out into the cold.

This has been the autumn of the cycle. If the reader takes seriously that the rape and death scene of Chapter III-4 was set in August and that the opening scene of Part V is set in September, then Part IV has occupied only the moment in between the end of one month and the beginning of another. Time has apparently stood still. The scattered references to time in Part IV speak of a hot September sun, wine-making in early October, and a hot July sun for the political season, all of which are tied to some extent to the negatives of human intercourse: despair, drunkenness, greed, brutality, hypocrisy and violence. However, the brevity of the references leaves the stage to the human element, which proves to be more violent and abusive than either hailstorms or hot sun. Having, as it were, allowed the human beings to show their true colors, the physical milieu can return to prominence in Part V, where, ironically, human conditions and actions now form the backdrop, while the climate occupies the foreground.

Fittingly, Part V begins in the filth of fermenting waste: the peasants are fertilizing their fields for fall planting. While the reader may find hope for future crops in the evident glorification of fertilization, the manure promises Jean only more human filth and degradation. As he passes through the following season of death, he will see not the beauty and hope of his first winter but only violence and murder. The cold, gray, damp calm of February, on the other hand, seems content to wait and to watch. Buteau finally manages to rape his sister-in-law, Françoise, though she is now Jean's pregnant wife, and her sister Lise helps him. Lise then pushes Françoise onto a scythe, and she and Buteau run away in terror, leaving Françoise to die (746-49). References to icy winds, ashen skies, sad skies, low, dark skies, and the empty, stripped fields are frequent, and the conjunction between this climate and the moral climate of the human beings is clear. Buteau and Lise try to cast off their chill in suffocating and burning Old Fouan, to keep him from telling what they did to Françoise and from reclaiming the money they stole. The final blow comes when the family and the whole village look with blind eyes upon these unjust and violent acts (chapters V-5 and V-6).

The solitary and indeed now alienated witness to these actions and reactions is Jean. Even prior to his wife's murder, the chill of despair had killed his idealism. He has come to see the earth for what it is: bare, cold soil hardened by rain and sun, raw and naked when it is turned up, and a great, sad calm in the distance where it is growing. The human beings, including himself, are now for him, too, precisely the scurrying insects noted earlier by the narrator's voice, hapless, hopeless, and loveless (736-37). They are as cold and hard as the earth, and their greed, brutality, and violence are as raw and naked. Jean's only remaining option is to go back to the army; if he cannot tolerate the role of soldier ant serving the soil, he can at least defend the land, and in so doing, he can have some say about his own life (811).

The final chapter of *The Land* centers on the burial of Old Fouan, surrounded even to the end by the frantic, angry buzz of human activity: the family squabbles over the old man's remaining money, others rage about grave sites, the priest comes only when forced to, and so on. The funeral-goers rush away before the grave is filled to watch a nearby farm burn. Jean alone stays by the open grave, musing on the brutality of "the bloody, stinking vermine that inhabits towns," a God who "doesn't give a damn," and the "huge mechanism of the stars and of the sun" which overwhelms and swallows up human existence (811).

The "mechanism" is of course the climate of Rognes and, by extension, of the entire earth. It is omnipresent in chapter V-6, where the focus is on the sun. The time of the stars has passed with the nighttime murder of Old Fouan and the night terrors of Jean as he struggled with his decision to leave Rognes. Now, a pale March sun reveals bits of blue sky and the still-frozen earth, that same cold cover which warmed the pregnant earth at the end of Part I. Beneath that cover, new life waits like sleepy-headed girls, as the narrator puts it, stretching and enjoying a few more moments in bed (796).

The sun does not warm Jean at first: he shivers at the sight of sowers in the field, once again spreading a golden wave of wheat seed across the land (797-98). He is warmed only at Old Fouan's grave, where the very lid of the old man's casket begins to look like wheat (805) and where, blinded by the pale sun, he is finally lulled into a gentle hope that is more acquiescence than even resignation (806-10). The land is at last triumphant over his idealism, as it controls the human insects that serve it: farms may burn and people may die, but, as Jean says, "You can't burn the land" (810). In fact, Jean now sees that along with the wheat seeds and the soil, the dead, no matter how they lived or died, are but necessary ingredients of the recipe that makes bread for the living and thus brings the land to its fulness (811). He, who cannot tolerate what is for him the living death of the Beauce, can only turn away and meet death on his own terms, in war.

Zola did not use any aspect of the imagery of climate to promote a science of nature or the politics of the French nation, nor simply as an ordering principle, nor as a convenient frame for a psychological tale. The psychological issues of *The Land* are clear; they concern almost exclusively the dilemmas of Jean and, to a much lesser extent, M. Hourdequin—both outsiders who must deal with their marginality if they are to survive in Rognes, and both unable to do so for reasons which are only partly psychological. The intense description of and constant preoccupation with physiological aspects of rural and agricultural matters—hardly avoidable given the subject—lend to the events of the novel an air of reality which sets off pseudo-scientific resonances designed rather to make the reader feel like a helpless witness to an immense and unjust natural disaster, non-human on the surface but in which human beings are clearly implicated.

Likewise, there is no external demand on *The Land* for the seasonal cycle—as for example the Christian bias in Dillard's *Pilgrim at Tinker Creek* (McIlroy 156). The cycle is indeed completely internal to the story, and it is carefully integrated into the action. Equally unlike the primarily psychological uses of summer imagery apparent in Rimbaud's *Une Saison en Enfer* (Amprimoz 56), Zola's uses of climate approach what has been called, in the work of still another poet, Valéry, "the language of the voluptuous imagination" (Lawler 405).[12] The author, in heightening the importance of both the form and the content of his story, thereby avoids the pitfalls common to many stories using nature imagery, which make nature the source of evil and thus put evil outside human beings (Wands 523), or which, vice versa, posit evil in humans and their societies and, finding nature pure and innocent, invent noble savages. For Zola, there is enough evil to go around, and human beings are more evil only insofar as they are victims of both nature and nurture.

In the final analysis, then, Zola differs most markedly from others who used and continue to use the imagery of climate in his fundamental attitude and in its formal realizations. He develops the seasonal cycle from winter through spring-summer-fall and back to winter in much the same way as Saint-Amant, in the sixteenth century (Merino 27). He also gives special consideration to winter as the season of death and renewal. But the tension between the renewal and the unrenewed human who does not fit into the natural cycle, who wants rather to reject acquiescence and resignation, makes all the difference between Zola and the Renaissance poet. Zola cannot end in joy at nature's bounty; his protagonist ends in the bitter realization that the foolish, greedy local peasants, not he, are blessed by nature, and that his choices are intolerable acquiescence or escape. So where Saint-Amant sees life overcoming death, Zola finds death triumphant over life.

In fact, there are only two seasons in Zola's novel: planting and harvesting, hope and despair. Human beings plant the seeds, at various times of the year, that will eventually turn into bread. When they harvest the seeds, the seeds have become as it were the blood of the bread—that which is essential to the life of the bread and of the human beings who, in consuming the bread, drink the blood of the plants. This is also the blood of the soil, indirectly, since it must be spilt upon the ground again to make more bread and more blood, and so on and on, round and round, like the seasonal cycle. But the cycle may continue without human intervention, as plants grow from bulbs beneath the surface, whose seeds remain in place, or from seeds on the surface fallen to the ground or carried by winds or by birds. Human beings intervene in their own interests, their actions impacting primarily their corner of the cosmos, and they live and die like other natural creatures. In their absence the other creatures continue to appear, thrive, and disappear, exactly as before, so that when the last human being has arrived at the last harvest, life goes on exactly as before. In conclusion, if climate plays a central role in *The Land,* death, the "ultimate scandal of naturalist fiction," is the central theme. Like climate, death is presented in stages, in terms of its causes. It moves from innocent to guilty, from the result of an act of nature to accidental homicide to second-degree and then first-degree murder. However, the most terrifying cause of death is not first-degree murder, or the hot sun that accompanies it, but the mindless living death, at once uncertain and predictable, like the weather, full of hope and despair, which afflicts the inhabitants of Rognes and thus inflicts upon them, and upon all with whom they come into contact, a moral as well as a physical death. To this extent, they are one with the climate; nature has, as Baguley says, drawn them into "essential compliance with its laws" and thus abolished their "distinct humanity" (216). So as the overall climate finally includes these human beings who are indistinguishable from the land, it also evokes and affirms the naturalistic vision of human existence.

Notes

1. See, for example, ms. N.a.f. 10.328.
2. This subtitle appears on the title page of volume 4 of the Pléiade edition of *Les Rougon-Macquart,* from which all of my citations of *La Terre (The Land)* are taken.
3. Robert 154, 203, 233, 465.
4. By "climate" I do not mean its figurative counterpart, as in intellectual, social, moral, or political climate—although I will have occasion to refer to these. I mean real, physical climate; but of course, since the climate at issue is part of a work of fiction, I truly mean such combinations of geographical features and seasonal weather patterns and events as Zola recreated or invented.

5. For a variety of views on several writers, all of whom approach this stance, see Kiesel 29-32, Kuizinga 388-89, McIlroy 157, Merino 27, and Youssef, 710.

6. In modern France, for instance, Rimbaud (Amprimoz 56), Mauriac (Garfitt 16-17), and Valéry (Lawler 400-01).

7. The theory had withered under scornful attacks by Voltaire (Fink 27).

8. The climate of the Beauce region southwest of Paris, the source of the setting for *The Land*, depends upon its flatness, its limestone foundation and relatively loose soil, its moderate elevation (500-1000 feet) and its situation between the North pole and the Equator. The average rainfall is twenty-four inches, more coming in the spring than in the winter, still more in the fall, and most with the summer storms. The average temperature is 53 degrees, winter lows and summer highs being moderate. Grain crops and forests are favored by this climate, whose seasonal variations are general and predictable. In the nineteenth century, the dominant crop was wheat, but other grain crops were common. All were and are very dependent upon the ebb and flow of weather conditions. This basic information is available in general reference works, such as *The Encyclopedia Britannica*.

9. See Robert 181, 234; Vernois 136.

10. Sutherland 434; see also Schama 305.

11. Robert (371) and Vernois (126) talk at length about the facts of the crisis of 1875-1890.

12. The comparison with poets and poetry is legitimized in the case of this novel by the facts that Zola himself spoke and wrote of his "poem of the land" (ms. fol. 400) and by the fact that many others have demonstrated the accuracy of this remark.

Works Cited

Amprimoz, Alexandre. "L'Eté rimbaldien: Mythe et réalité textuelle." *Dalhousie French Studies* 14 (Spring-Summer 1988): 52-63.

Baguley, David. *Naturalist Fiction: The Entropic Vision*. Cambridge: Cambridge University Press, 1990.

Fink, Gonthier-Louis. "De Bouhours . . . Herder." *Recherches germaniques* 15 (1985): 3-62.

Garfitt, J. S. T. "Distortion of Time in Mauriac's *Le Désert de l'amour*." *French Studies Bulletin* (Spring 1987): 16-17.

Jareño, Ernesto. "Enumeraciones fijas y algunos ejemplos de series léxicas limitadas." *Archivum* 31 (1981): 417-49.

Kiesel, Frédéric. "Anne-Marie Kegels: saisons et métamorphoses." *Revue Générale* 5 (May 1984): 27-33.

Kuizinga, Donna. "Saint-Amant's Seasonal Cycle: A Baroque Myth." *The French Review* 56 (February 1983): 385-92.

Lawler, James. "'Eté, roche d'air pur . . . .'" *Baudelaire, Mallarmé, Valéry: New Essays in Honour of Lloyd Austin*. Eds. Malcolm Bowie, Alison Fairlie, and Alison Finch. Cambridge: Cambridge University Press, 1982. 398-410.

McIlroy, Gary. "'The Sparer Climate for Which I Longed': *Pilgrim at Tinker Creek* and the Spiritual Imperatives of Fall." *The Thoreau Quarterly* 16 (Summer-Fall 1984): 156-61.

Merino, Jane. "The Four Seasons According to Saint-Amant: A Semiotic Approach." *Papers on French Seventeenth-Century Literature* 8 (1981): 23-28.

Robert, Guy. *"La Terre" d'Emile Zola*. Paris: Les Belles Lettres, 1952. Translations are mine.

Sklar, Judith. "Virtue in a Bad Climate: Good Men and Good Citizens in Montesquieu's *L'Esprit des lois*." *Enlightenment Studies in Honour of Lester G. Crocker*. Eds. Alfred Bingham and Virgil Topazio. Oxford: Voltaire Foundation, 1979. 315-28.

Sutherland, Donald. "Weather and Peasantry of Upper Brittany, 1780-1789." *Climate and History.* Eds. T. M. L. Wigley, M. J. Ingram, and G. Farmer. Cambridge: Cambridge University Press, 1981. 434-49.

Schama, Simon. *Citizen: A Chronicle of the French Revolution.* New York: Vintage Books, 1989.

Tintner, Adeline. "Millet and Zola's *La Terre.*" *Trivium* 21 (1986): 95-113.

Vernois, Paul. *Le Roman rustique de George Sand à Ramuz.* Paris: Nizet, 1962.

Wands, John. "The Theory of Climate in the English Renaissance and *Mundus Alter et Idem.*" *Acta Conventus Neo-Latini Sanctandreani.* Ed. I. D. McFarlane. Binghampton, N.Y.: Medieval and Renaissance Text Studies, 1986. 519-29.

Youssef, Zobeldah. "Le Spectacle de l'hiver dans la correspondance de Madame de Sévigné," *Papers on French Seventeenth-Century Literature* 15 (1988): 701-20.

Zola, Emile. *The Naturalist Novel.* Trans. Belle M. Sherman. Montreal: Harvest House, 1964.

_____. Manuscript at the Bibliothèque Nationale, Paris, Nouvelles acquisitions françaises 10.328. Citations taken from filmed copy at Texas Tech University library. Translations are mine.

_____. *Les Rougon-Macquart.* Ed. Henri Mitterand. 4th ed. Paris: Gallimard, 1966. Translations are mine.

 # The Role of Climate in Twentieth-Century Spanish American Fiction

George R. McMurray

The topic of climate in Spanish American fiction evokes an almost overwhelming number of titles to anyone who has read extensively from the literature of our southern neighbors. This, of course, is hardly surprising, given the vast geographical area under scrutiny and the astonishing variety of settings within the purview of Spanish American writers. Indeed, climate and its effects are alluded to in works ranging from the chronicles of early settlers in the New World to nineteenth-century masterworks such as Sarmiento's *Facundo,* in which nature and climate are part of barbarism, and Jorge Isaac's *María,* whose setting, el Valle del Cauca in Colombia, reflects a sentimental phase of romanticism. In the present century climate assumes an even greater role with the vivid descriptions of the regionalist novel. In *Doña Bárbara* for example, the untamed plains of Venezuela, with their *tolvaneras* or dust storms, challenge the strength and tenacity of ranchers. Similarly, the storms on the Argentine pampas test the mettle of Sabio Cáceres in *Don Segundo Sombra.* The ravages of cruel nature and adverse weather conditions in *The Vortex* contribute to the dramatic backdrop for the struggle against the rubber barons of Colombia's Amazonian jungle. And in the Andean highlands, *Huasipungo, Broad and Alien Is the World,* and *Altiplano* (a lesser-known Bolivian novel by Raúl Botelho Gozalves) depict the harsh living conditions in that region exacerbated by frigid blasts of thin air, cloudbursts, flash floods and, in the case of *Altiplano,* extreme drought. Still in the context of regionalism, *The Underdogs* reflects the perpetual drought in the northern Mexican desert with its dramatic allusions to craggy mountain peaks devoid of vegetation, treeless plains, and clouds of dust stirred up by men on horseback. And, finally in this introduction, mention should be made of Horacio Quiroga's tales set in the jungles of Misiones, Argentina, where heat and humidity reinforce the terror of death.

The first work I should like to treat in more detail is Martín Luis Guzmán's *La sombra del caudillo* (*The Shadow of the Tyrant*), a "roman á clef" written in the late 1920s to dramatize the betrayal of the Mexican Revolution by corrupt politicians. In the first part of this novel, General Aguirre, the minister of war in the caudillo's cabinet, has a rendezvous with Rosario in Chapultepec Park, where he is driven by his chauffeur. Just prior to the young lady's arrival Aguirre promises his friend Axkaná, who represents Aguirre's conscience, that he will not seduce the innocent young Rosario. Rosario's subsequent refusal to get into Aguirre's Cadillac leads to their leisurely walk through the park. Suddenly, about 4:00 o'clock in the afternoon, a rainstorm forces them into Aguirre's limousine, an act followed by Rosario's seduction. Because Rosario scarcely appears throughout the rest of the novel, the reader is likely to question the reason for this scene. A possible explanation, for which I owe Juan Bruce Novoa, is that Rosario's seduction foreshadows Aguirre's subsequent behavior, that is, his categorical statement that he is not a candidate for president and then his acceptance of the nomination as a result of events at least in part beyond his control.[1] But more important here is the summer afternoon shower, typical in Mexico City, which provides Guzmán with a means of suggesting Aguirre's weakness (and foreshadowing his eventual downfall) in the opening pages of the novel.

Two of the best Spanish American writers of their generation are Elena Poniatowska and Antonio Skármeta, both of whom have used weather conditions in Europe to reinforce mood. Poniatowska's *Dear Diego* is a testimonial novel narrated by Diego Rivera's Russian common-law wife, Angelina Beloff, who lived with the famous painter in Paris before and during World War I. Beloff's letters, supposedly written in Paris between October 1921 and July 1922, after Rivera returned to his homeland, exude a bleak atmosphere of solitude due in part to her desire to join Diego in Mexico (he had promised to send her money to make the trip) and in part to the death of their infant child Dieguito from meningitis. Beloff's allusions to the gray Parisian winter become a kind of leitmotif, underscoring her loneliness and contrasting with the blue skies of Mexico she imagines and longs to see firsthand.

In a somewhat similar vein, Skármeta's *Burning Patience* depicts Pablo Neruda as Chile's ambassador in Paris toward the end of his life and his poignant desire, expressed in a letter to his friend Mario, to hear sounds from his home in Isla Negra on the Chilean coast. Immediately thereafter, Mario, who has learned to appreciate poetry from his mentor, writes his "Ode to the Snow Over Neruda in Paris," which uses poetic images of snow to express his feelings for Neruda. This ode ends as follows: "Please, pale beauty, fall gently upon Neruda in Paris. Dress him up in your white admiral's suit and carry him in your small boat to this port where he is so much missed" (85).

Skármeta's lesser-known novel, *Nothing Happened,* which takes place in West Berlin, is narrated by Lucho, a fourteen-year-old boy whose family sought exile in Germany after the 1973 military coup in Chile. This tale of a youth's acceptance into a foreign culture comes to a climax when, in a dispute over a girl, Lucho seriously injures a German boy and is forced into a fight with the boy's brother, Michael. Under increasingly cloudy skies Michael drives the apprehensive Lucho on his motorcycle to an isolated spot in the city where they engage in a hotly disputed fist-fight. The fight ends when the enraged and all-but-defeated Lucho knocks Michael unconscious with a rock. About this time the sky unleashes a downpour, causing Michael to regain consciousness and inducing both youths to forget their dispute in an Italian restaurant over wine and pizza. The threatening clouds and sudden storm in this sequence of events serve two purposes. First, they lend greater suspense to the entire climactic episode; and second, on a more mythical level, they signal the demise of Lucho's childhood and his rite of passage to manhood.

Carlos Fuentes' "Chac Mool" is another story in which rain plays a mythical role. In this well-known *ficción* we are led to believe that a pre-Hispanic rain god unleashes torrents of water onto the Mexican capital while, at the same time, a statue of the god comes to life, driving Filiberto, one of the narrators, to Acapulco and to his death by drowning. At the end of the story the first narrator, a friend of Filiberto's, discovers that Chac Mool has come to life, replacing Filiberto in his home. As John Brushwood has commented, this fantasy conveys Fuentes' theme of *mexicanidad* (Mexican-ness), inasmuch as the story refers to both Mexican myth and contemporary Mexican life (the vitalized Chac Mool shows superficial characteristics of modern culture). But along with the central figure of the rain god, it is the torrential rains that link Mexico's present and past, thus reinforcing Fuentes' conviction (and theme) that concealed beneath the veneer of modern Western culture, Mexico's indigenous myths remain vibrantly alive in the twentieth century and ready to burst onto the surface at any moment. Although climate hardly stands out as a major ingredient in Jorge Luis Borges's abstract, cerebral stories, "The Gospel According to Mark" is indeed based on a climatic phenomenon, namely, the biblical flood. The setting is a ranch near Buenos Aires where a kindly medical student, Baltasar Espinosa, is spending his summer vacation. While his cousin, the owner of the ranch, is in the city on a business trip, a severe rainstorm causes a flood, isolating Espinosa, the foreman Gutre, and Gutre's son and daughter. Espinosa finds an English Bible containing the family chronicle of the Gutres (originally Guthries), which reveals that they are a mixture of Scottish and Indian blood, their Scottish ancestors having arrived in Argentina early in the nineteenth century. The chronicle ceased in the 1870s when the Gutres no longer knew how to write. The foreman and his children are illiterate, know no English, can barely speak Spanish, and have no religious faith. We are told, however, that the rigid fanaticism of the Calvinist and the superstitions of the pampa Indian survive in their blood.

Because of a leak in the roof of their house, the Gutres move into the main house with Espinosa for the duration of the storm. Every night after dinner Espinosa, who is an eloquent speaker, reads to them a portion of the Gospel According to St. Mark, a story that holds a mysterious fascination for them. The respect and affection Espinosa has earned from the Gutres through his repeated reading of "The Gospel According to St. Mark" is enhanced when he cures a pet lamb injured on a strand of barbed wire.

One night Espinosa dreams of the Flood and imagines he hears the hammer blows of carpenters building the Ark. Upon awakening, he learns that the rain has damaged the roof of the toolshed, which the Gutres supposedly have set about to repair. The next day Gutre asks Espinosa if Christ allowed himself to be crucified for the sake of all men and, though a free thinker, Espinosa feels obliged to answer in the affirmative. That afternoon, while taking a nap, Espinosa again imagines he hears a persistent hammering. When he gets up, the Gutres ask for his blessing, then spit at him and push him toward the back part of the house. Through the open door to the toolshed, Espinosa can see that it is without a roof, because the Gutres have taken down the beams to make a cross.

"The Gospel According to Mark" lends itself to various interpretations, one of which is that time is circular, an idea with special appeal to Borges. Thus the biblical flood recurs, but instead of having its mythical purifying effect, it ironically signals a return to savagery when the Gutres intend to crucify Espinosa, an obvious Christ figure, in the hope of achieving redemption by assuming his virtues. Borges's depiction of the Flood and its ironic aftermath suggests that although specific circumstances change, religious fanaticism is permanently imbedded in the human psyche.

Rain also plays a role in Juan Rulfo's "We're Very Poor," but this tale takes the form of a rambling monologue by an unnamed adolescent whose sister Tacha has lost her cow in a flood. Now without a dowry to attract a suitor, Tacha is in danger of following in the footsteps of her older sisters, both of whom have become prostitutes. Their ruin, the loss of Tacha's cow, and Tacha's inevitable fate are all somehow connected to the image of the swollen river, which runs throughout the story as if to emphasize the symbiotic relationship between the characters and hostile nature. Thus in the final lines

Tacha is described with her tear-covered face, "as if the river had gotten inside her" (85) and her maturing breasts bouncing up and down, starting her on the road to ruin.

Unlike "We're Very Poor," the majority of Rulfo's tales depict the dry, parched landscape of Jalisco, leaving a taste of dust in the reader's mouth and, as in the case of the swollen river and Tacha, reflecting the barren lives of the characters. In "Luvina," the name of a poverty-stricken village evoked by the narrator who spent an unspecified number of years there, the wind whistling through the streets and ramshackle buildings becomes a haunting image of decay. Laden with a volcanic sand, this wind withers virtually all vegetation, rips roofs from houses, and filters under doors, "until you feel it boiling inside of you as if it was going to remove the hinges of your very bones" (112). Rulfo utilizes the flood in "We're Very Poor" and the wind in "Luvina" not only as unifying structuring devices, but also as conveyors of his highly pessimistic Weltanschauung.

In *Pedro Páramo*, also by Juan Rulfo, the contrast between the live Comala of the past and the dead Comala of the present, a community obsessed with its lifetime sins, provides the novel with luminous poetic passages and one of its major themes. Thus the Comala of the past, evoked by the voices of Dolores Preciado and Pedro Páramo, is a kind of paradise characterized by rain, green vegetation, and kites propelled by the wind. But with the demise of the town, houses collapse, everything dries up and the wind ceases to blow, turning Comala into an inferno, a place so hot that when people die and go to hell, they come back for their blankets. Rulfo's antithetical visions of Comala as paradise and hell, together with his references to sin, suggest that a major theme of *Pedro Páramo* is man's fall from grace.

Though less prominent than in Rulfo's fiction, climate also plays a role in José Donoso's stories. In "China," for example, a rainy evening in a crowded working-class district of Santiago stimulates the imagination of the child-narrator, who is convinced that his mother has taken him to China. The theme of the disintegrating family is expressed in "Summertime" by a mansion that has fallen in ruins after years of wind, rain and neglect. The wind on the sparsely populated Chilean pampas emerges as a symbol of loneliness in "The Dane's Place," whose protagonist is an ex-prostitute terrified at the prospect of being left alone after her daughter's marriage.

But it is in "The Güero," which means the blond, that climatic factors assume greater prominence in Donoso's short fiction. Here the setting is a tropical Mexican village, Tlacotlalpan, where an American botany professor (Mr. Howland), his wife, and their blond, nine-year-old son Mike live for an extended period of time. Being exceptionally rational people, the Howlands hope and fully expect that Mike will grow up to be just like them, free of ignorance and superstition. Exactly the opposite occurs, however, when Mike becomes infatuated with tales of a white god and, on a stormy night, leads a group of his Indian friends up the river in search of the mythical deity. The boat capsizes and the boys all drown during the storm. The title "The Guero" suggests the physical contrast between Mike and the other boys in Tlacotlalpan, where the searing tropical sun and the climactic storm, symbols of primitive instinct, help to convey Donoso's major theme, namely, that in comparison to the instinctive side of human nature, rational thought (embodied by Mr. and Mrs. Howland) is a mere tip of the iceberg.

Upon considering the theme of climate in Spanish American literature, many readers of contemporary fiction would focus first of all on Gabriel García Márquez's oeuvre. The hyperbolic rains in *One Hundred Years of Solitude,* which remind us of the purifying biblical flood and which cause Fernanda's day-long tirade directed at her husband, would perhaps first come to mind. Even more graphic in their descriptions, however, are *Monologue of Isabel Watching It Rain in Macondo,* depicting the protagonist's physical and psychological disintegration during a monotonous five-day rain, and "Tuesday's Siesta," whose masterful open ending portrays an impoverished woman and her young daughter bravely confronting the hostile gazes of town citizens under a blazing tropical sun.

One could write a lengthy article about García Márquez's treatment of climate, if indeed it has not already been done, but I will treat in some detail only two of the Colombian master's books, *The Tale of a Shipwrecked Sailor* and *No One Writes to the Colonel. The Tale of a Shipwrecked Sailor,* which can be read as a testimonial novel, presents two themes, both related to climate. The first of these is, obviously, the ten-day-long struggle of a young sailor, Luis Velasco, against the elements after he is swept overboard from the Colombian destroyer, the Caldas, during rough seas in the Caribbean. Emerging as leitmotifs, the adverse climatic conditions include the wind, which creates huge waves that turn the young man's raft over on two occasions; the blazing sun, which he repeatedly refers to as his implacable enemy because of the blisters on much of his body; the torrents of rain that drastically lower his body temperature; and the undertow that almost prevents him from reaching the beach where he is rescued. This work is fraught with dramatic tension and shifting moods, much of which derives from the protagonist's reactions to weather conditions. Thus, when the sea is calm, Velasco's level of despair decreases; when his raft is overturned by high waves, he struggles bravely to remain afloat, on one occasion falling off the raft and, virtually in panic, momentarily losing sight of it; and when he finally sights land, he goes into a rage, thinking that the sun has played tricks on him by presenting him with a mirage.

The second theme of this exciting tale is García Márquez's confrontation with the corrupt government of Colombia, which is provoked by the discrepancy between Luis Velasco's version of the weather in the Caribbean before the accident and the official version published by the government. Upon interviewing Velasco for *El Espectador* (the tale was published first as a series of newspaper articles), García Márquez was struck by the young man's revelation that the accident had not been caused by a storm, as officials had declared, but rather that the eight sailors had been swept overboard because the naval destroyer was carrying unevenly stowed contraband goods from Mobile, Alabama, such as washing machines, stoves, and television sets, causing the boat to list. When the government denied the young sailor's assertions, photographs showing crates of the contraband goods on board the ship were published in *El Espectador*, eventually leading to the newspaper's closure by the Colombian dictator Rojas Pinilla.

But it is García Márquez's narrative discourse that best demonstrates his confrontation with corrupt power over this vital question of weather. Thus, instead of explicitly accusing the Colombian navy of allowing contraband goods on board the Caldas, the author incorporates into his story visual images reminding the reader that such is the case. For example, Velasco states that when he was washed overboard, he was attempting to sleep on deck surrounded by the crates of appliances, thinking that they would protect him from the waves splashing onto the boat. And soon thereafter he found himself in the rough sea, clinging frantically to one of many floating crates around him before managing to reach the raft on which he would spend the next ten days.

The action of *No One Writes to the Colonel*, García Márquez's first masterpiece, takes place in a tropical Colombian town between October (during the winter or rainy season) and December (the beginning of the summer or dry season). Alluded to repeatedly throughout the novel, these climatic conditions provide its structural underpinnings in several respects. The colonel's intestinal problems, according to him, are caused by the depressing winter rains. Death and "la violencia" are referred to again and again during the depressing months of October and November. And during the winter the colonel's grinding poverty (along with his wife's insistence) almost induces him to sell the fighting cock, a symbol of hope. But with the advent of December, the brilliant sunshine and the success of the colonel's fighting cock in a trial bout make not only his spirits soar, but those of the entire pueblo as well. This memorable character ultimately emerges as an absurd hero who struggles against overwhelming odds, including the winter rains, until he defiantly utters his famous last word.

In several Spanish American works of fiction that come to mind, climate stands out as a major factor in the creation of humor. A prime example is *One Hundred Years of Solitude*, in which the prissy, aristocratic Fernanda del Carpio, a cachaca or inlander from Bogotá, is like a fish out of water among the natives of Macondo, especially her fun-loving husband Aureliano Segundo Buendía. Thus Fernanda becomes the butt of many hilarious episodes based on absurdities such as her golden chamber pot, the calendar her confessor has marked with many days of sexual abstinence, the neatly sewed hole in the front of her long wedding-night nightgown, and the arrival of her revered father bubbling in the heat of his medieval coffin. García Márquez, whose dislike for Bogotá is legendary, suggests in the gloomy scenes of his novel set in the Colombian highlands that the cold, dreary climate, in contrast to Macondo's steamy tropical temperatures, is at least in part responsible for the dichotomy in temperament between Colombians.

Another example of humor stemming from climatic differences is found in Captain Pantoja and the Secret Service, by Mario Vargas Llosa, who I suspect was influenced by the rollicking and at times grotesque humor in *One Hundred Years of Solitude*. Indeed, vague comparisons could be made between Fernanda del Carpio and the straitlaced Pantaleón. Like Fernanda, Pantaleón elicits our guffaws when he suddenly finds himself in a very different, sexually-charged environment. Thus, upon arriving in the scorching, tropical city of Iquitos at midday, he desires sexual intercourse from his shocked wife immediately after they are settled in their hotel. The humor here derives from the effects of the tropical heat on Pantaleón's libido, especially in view of the fact that neither he, nor his commanding officers, nor his wife, nor the reader anticipates his sudden impulsive behavior, all of which only accentuates the importance of climate in this comic novel.

Isabel Allende's *Eva Luna* also contains resonances of *One Hundred Years of Solitude*, especially in its style and narrative point of view. Less interested than García Márquez in climatic phenomena, Allende nevertheless, in at least one passage, evokes the hyperbole and humor of the Colombian master. While serving in the home of an aging couple, Eva Luna is befriended by an older servant, Elvira, who has purchased a coffin in order to avoid her dreaded fate of burial in a common grave. Many years after Eva Luna has lost track of her friend, a week-long rainstorm causing a devastating flood is brought to a halt by the prayers of worshippers, despite the predictions of meteorologists that the rain would last another nine days. Meanwhile Eva Luna sees on television pictures of a casket that has floated into the center of the city and, inside the casket, her friend Elvira announcing that she has been saved from the flood by her "ark."

But the most absurd treatment of climate that I have come across is "And We Sold the Rain," a short story by one of Costa Rica's most talented writers, Carmen Naranjo. Reminiscent of a well-known episode depicting gringo imperialism in *The Autumn of the Patriarch,* this tale describes a poverty-stricken nation whose only natural resource is rain. The solution to this problem comes when the country hosts the "Miss Underveloped" beauty contest, and a contestant from an oil-rich, desert kingdom returns home and informs her emir of the fabulous rains falling daily on the poverty-stricken nation she has just visited. The emir immediately instructs his foreign trade minister to arrange an agreement whereby a series of aqueducts between the two nations will bring water to the desert emirate. At first an economic boom brings prosperity to the poor, rain-soaked nation, but when the International Monetary Fund begins to demand interest payments on back loans, more and more aqueducts must be built for the exportation of water. Eventually the country runs out of its precious resource and dries up, causing all its citizens to float via the aqueducts to the thriving emirate, which in the meantime has become a green paradise. In a few years, however, oil prices plunge, and when the emirate is forced to borrow heavily and then default on its loan payments, the IMF takes possession of the aqueducts, and the flow of water is cut off.

The last work I should like to mention has little to do with climate except for its metaphoric title. *Tiempo nublado,* by Octavio Paz, is a collection of essays published in 1983, in which Paz discusses recent world developments, especially those of the 1970s. The book's title, which means cloudy weather, expresses Paz's vision of the world at the time the essays were written, a world he views as endangered by pressing issues such as overpopulation, the depletion of energy supplies, environmental pollution, ruinous economic recessions, the proliferation of fanatical ideologies, and the plague of international terrorism. As a means of coming to grips with these issues, Paz stresses the importance of democracy because only this form of government gives its citizens the right to criticize freely and thus effect necessary social and political change. But while clearly preferring the United States to the totalitarian Soviet Union, Paz does not hesitate to attack the United States for its political intervention in Latin America, especially in Nicaragua and El Salvador. He also strongly criticizes both Europe and the United States for their emphasis on hedonistic consumerism and individual gain at the expense of civic virtues and moral responsibilities to the rest of the world. But Tiempo nublado is not basically the pessimistic book its title suggests. Rather, its emphasis on the need for clear, critical thinking, freedom of expression, and openness to change represents Paz's existential philosophy and fundamental hope in an increasingly dangerous world.

The foregoing examples suggest that climate is an especially important element in Spanish American literature. Indeed, the subject is so vast that much must remain unsaid. I have attempted to present a smattering of the roles played by climate in a few selected literary works. These roles range from adversary to mankind *(Story of a Shipwrecked Sailor* and "We're Very Poor") and political commentary ("And They Sold the Rain") to conveyer of theme ("Chac Mool," "Luvina," "The Guero," "The Gospel According to Mark," *Dear Diego* and *Pedro Páramo*), structuring device *(No One Writes to the Colonel),* creator of dramatic tension *(Nothing Happened)* and source of hyperbole and comedy *(One Hundred Years of Solitude, Captain Pantoja and the Secret Service* and *Eva Luna).* The physical environment of the New World has been a major factor in the shaping of Spanish American literature, including its pervasive, if somewhat simplistic, theme of civilization against barbarism. While climate remains an untamed adversary to mankind in Spanish American fiction of the present century, it has more interesting and more subtle roles as well.

Note

1. See Juan Bruce-Novoa, "Martín Luis Guzmán's Necessary Overtures," 63-83.

Works Cited

Bruce-Novoa, Juan. "Martín Luis Guzmán's Necessary Overtures," *Discurso Literario* 4.1 (1986): 63-83.

Rulfo, Juan. *The Burning Plain and Other Stories.* Trans. George D. Schade. Austin: University of Texas Press, 1967.

Skármeta, Antonio. *Burning Patience.* Trans. Katherine Silver. New York: Pantheon Books, 1987.

 # The Endless Rains of Death and Desolation in García Márquez's Short Stories

Clementina R. Adams

García Márquez's short stories are strongly influenced by two primary elements: climate conditions characteristic of his homeland and nostalgia for his childhood years. Both elements have had a decisive influence on the content, mood, setting and treatment of his work.

Aracataca, García Márquez's birthplace, is located on the northern coast of Colombia. This town and many other towns in the State of Magdalena and on the Atlantic coast, such as Barranquilla, appear in the writer's fiction. Their location close to the sea and to the equator has made their atmospheric conditions unique in relation to other coastal towns. In that area, there are only two main seasons: the dry season, from November to April; and the rainy season, from April to November, with a refreshing break in June, which is usually known as "el veranillo de San Juan" (short summer of Saint John).

During the rainy season, the heat and dampness become unbearable and suffocating. In addition, the rain becomes intolerable and frightening, especially since floods and destruction are frequent in some villages. Catastrophes usually accompany those endless rains.

To García Márquez, human feelings and a sense of existence are intertwined with perceptions of climatological conditions. In his works, the heat and dampness of hot days are usually associated with feelings of anger, anxiety and skepticism, but they can also represent the drowsiness and stupor of an empty, paralyzed and hopeless life, full of desperation and anxiety which, in spite of it all, is heavy with "existence."

The setting for most of García Márquez's writings is "Macondo," a small coastal town that André Jansen described as a "pueblecito ignorado de los geógrafos pero muy parecido a la aldea donde vivió su infancia, entre los platanales a orillas de un río por donde llega cada semana un barco con las escasas noticias del mundo exterior, cuando lo permite la estación de las lluvias" (128).

Macondo can further be described as a poor community filled with sensuality, vices, lust, unbearable heat and desperation, and punished with wars, injustice, bad luck, and death. Fernando Ayala Poveda, in his *Manual de Literatura*, says:

> Del mismo modo como Shakespeare, Cervantes, Balzac, Tolstoi y otros demiurgos tienen un mundo personal, regido por una sociedad, una ecología y una humanidad, asimismo, Gabriel García Márquez ha podido crear un universo totalizante que es análogo al universo real (333-34).

García Márquez's three volumes of short stories: *Eyes of a Blue Dog, Big Mama's Funeral,* and *The Incredible and Sad Tale of Innocent Eréndira and Her Heartless Grandmother*, contain abundant descriptions of hot dry days, dry burning winds, and the drowsiness caused by excessive heat. There are also descriptions of fierce, suffocating, and destructive winds.

In "The Incredible and Sad Tale of Innocent Eréndira," there are several allusions to the winds of misfortune and disaster; for example:

> The wind became drier as they headed north and the sun was fiercer than the wind. It was hard to breathe because of the heat and dust inside the closed-in truck (297; this and subsequent references to García Márquez's short stories come from his *Collected Stories*).

> The house was away from everything, in the heart of the desert, next to a settlement with miserable and burning streets where the goats committed suicide from desolation when the wind of misfortune blew (264).

From *Big Mama's Funeral,* the story "Tuesday Siesta" presents a variety of concrete examples of the effects of the heat and the intolerable humidity on people's habits, feelings and reactions: "A band was playing a lively tune under the oppressive sun" (100). "A dry, burning wind came in the window, together with the locomotive's whistle and the clatter of the old cars" (101). "The town was floating in the heat . . . . At that hour, weighted down by drowsiness, the town was taking a siesta" (101).

Another reference to the shocking effect of heat comes from the story, "There are no Thieves in This Town": "A man was sleeping sprawled in a rocking chair, with his lips and legs wide apart, in the hotel lobby. Everything was paralyzed in the noonday heat" (115).

The heat sometimes appears as a powerful element capable of changing people's feelings and even their concepts of things or situations to the point of generating skepticism, as in the case of the priest who said how inscrutable

God's ways were, and who, according to the author, said it not so much out of conviction but partly because of his experience and partly because of the heat.

It seems that the heat takes possession of the characters, submerging them in a kind of stupor that dominates their decision-making capabilities. "One Day After Saturday," from *Big Mama's Funeral*, presents a good description of these types of emotional-mental states: "Dozing on the hotel veranda, dulled by the sweltering heat, he had not stopped to think about the gravity of his situation" (169).

Because of the intense and lengthy periods of rain usually accompanied by floodings of small towns, bringing death and suffering, this natural phenomenon is constantly associated, in García Márquez's stories, with death, and with feelings of desolation, fear, despair, and solitude. In the story, "The Other Side of Death," from *Eyes of a Blue Dog*, García Márquez says: "The cold of his hands intensified, making him feel the presence of the formaldehyde in his arteries; as if the dampness of the courtyard had come into him down to the bones" (18).

Similar examples appear in "Big Mama's Funeral":

> All the splendor which she had dreamed of on the balcony of her house during her heat-induced insomnia was fulfilled by those forty-eight glorious hours during which all the symbols of the age paid homage to her memory. (199)

From *Eyes of a Blue Dog*, the story, "Eva is Inside Her Cat," also describes feelings of loneliness and fear: "That night the night of her passage had been colder than usual and she was alone in the house, martyrized by insomnia. No one disturbed the silence, and the smell that came from the garden was a smell of fear" (27).

Most of these short stories abound in descriptions of people's feelings about the rain with its "monotonous and pitiless rhythm," creating feelings of impotence, misery, sadness, chaos, desperation, paralysis, and resignation. Descriptions of these feelings and feelings of unwilling resignation are found in the pages of the stories, "Monologue of Isabel Watching It Rain in Macondo," and in "A Very Old Man With Enormous Wings."

García Márquez reflects on how the rain comes first as a refreshing change after seven months of scorching heat. However, after a time of constant monotonous dripping accompanied by a sad gray sky, the rain starts penetrating the senses and all those other feelings of anxiety and desperation start to surface.

From *Eyes of a Blue Dog*, the story "Monologue of Isabel Watching It Rain in Macondo" has interesting observations of changed or altered feelings.

But without our noticing it, the rain was penetrating too deeply into our senses . . . "I think they had more than enough water during the night," my stepmother said. And I noticed that she had stopped smiling and that her joy of the previous day had changed during the night into a lax and tedious seriousness (90).

We were paralyzed, drugged by the rain, given over to the collapse of nature with a peaceful and resigned attitude (92).

From *The Incredible and Sad Tale of Innocent Eréndira and Her Heartless Grandmother,* the story "A Very Old Man With Enormous Wings" describes feelings of hopelessness and desolation which mirror the rain and gloom:

The world had been sad since Tuesday. Sea and sky were a single ash-gray thing and the sands of the beach, which on March nights glimmered like powdered light, had become a stew of mud and rotten shellfish (203).

During the prolonged rainy season, the characters in García Márquez's stories often start feeling nostalgic for the good days of the dry season, dominated by a clear blue sky and a warming sun. Such nostalgic feelings occur many times in the story "Monologue of Isabel Watching It Rain in Macondo" from *Eyes of a Blue Dog.* The following passages exemplify this mood:

It looks as if it will never clear. And I remembered the months of heat. I remembered August, those long and awesome siestas in which we dropped down to die under the weight of the hour, our clothes sticking to our bodies, hearing outside the insistent and dull buzzing of the hour that never passed . . . . I remember the August nights in whose wondrous silence nothing could be heard except the millinery sound that the earth makes as it spins on its rusty, unoiled axis. (91)

Much has been written about García Márquez's sources of inspiration. Some critics believe that his inspiration comes from his rich and unique imagination, and others suggest that it comes from his ability to observe and to listen carefully to stories told by others (Apuleyo, McNerney, Vargas Llosa, and Williams, among others).

Weather conditions can trigger emotions and feelings experienced in the past, especially in childhood. Those nostalgic feelings appear to have been a source of inspiration for García Márquez. John Benson corroborates this theory, stating that García Márquez's source of inspiration comes from his nostalgia for the past (paper presented at MIFLC, October 1990).

Pedro Simón Martínez notes that García Márquez's memories of his grandmother's stories appear very frequently in his writings. Through them, he is able to indulge his nostalgia by retelling his remembrances of childhood and of the social life and customs of the times. Martínez quotes García Márquez's description of his grandmother: "La anciana tenía vena, y 'ella hablaba así.' Se oye a menudo su voz lejana en la trastienda, recordando a García Márquez el mundo mágico de la infancia en que creció, que transfigura a tantas de sus mejores páginas" (19-20).

Evidence of García Márquez's nostalgia for his childhood provides a strong basis for the notion that the geographical, social, and climatological conditions of his birthplace and childhood had a great deal to do with the special quality of his inspiration, and became integral elements of his short stories, affecting and sustaining moods which enhanced the thoughts and actions of his characters.

García Márquez's work is very much a reflection of his childhood on the Caribbean coast of Colombia, an area saturated by heat and humidity during the dry season and full of endless and depressing rains during the rainy season. The memories of his childhood are equally saturated with magic and unusual events, counterbalanced by violence and oppression. It was a world of folklore and fantasy, but also of desperation, suffering and injustice for the poor and the weak. Religious beliefs gave them hope and were, for many, their only way of surviving. Perhaps because these elements appeared in his grandmother's stories, García Márquez sometimes adds touches of mystery, magic, and witchery to his work, and frequently the climatological elements to play an important part in these events. Especially noteworthy is his treatment of winds, often associated with witchery and bad luck. Winds symbolize change which, in García Márquez's stories, is rarely for the good.

The following illustrative quotes are from "The Incredible and Sad Tale of Innocent Eréndira and Her Heartless Grandmother."

> A wind as fierce as the wind of misfortune shook their burlap habits and their rough beards and they were barely able to stand on their feet. (280)

> That night, a little after seven o'clock, Eréndira was combing her grandmother's hair when the wind of her misfortune blew again. (292)

Wind not only portends misfortune but creates it, making it a malevolent force, unlike the rain, which brings both benefits and disaster. From "The Incredible and Sad Tale of Innocent Eréndira and Her Heartless Grandmother":

> It was such a terrible storm that the rain was all mixed in with sea water, and the next morning the house was full of fish and snails and your grandfather Amadís, may he rest in peace, saw a glowing manta ray floating through the air. (278)

Extreme weather conditions are reflective of the socio-political climate of García Márquez's homeland. The excessive rains, characteristic of the rainy season in the northern coastal area of Colombia, as well as the excessive heat of the dry season, constitute a quasi-autonomous soul embedded in García Márquez's short stories, which faithfully reflect how the dry hot season comes as a relief from the intense winter rains, and how soon it provokes feelings of anger, insomnia, daydreaming, and desperation.

Characters appear particularly vulnerable, both to climatic change and to the lack of it. At the end of an intensely hot dry season, people yearn once again for the rainy season. Feelings toward the weather often resemble or reflect their feelings toward the social-political climate. The possibility of social or political change is initially welcome as any new season might be but, after a time, people begin to realize that they are once again in a purgatory of endless waiting and, once again, they yearn for the new social change as much as they yearned for the changing season.

Nostalgia for the past blends with concern for social and political realities in García Márquez's short stories. In them he combines images of the past filled with beauty, mystery, apocalyptic symbols, and tropical folklore with realistic settings that represent the social, religious, and political life of his country.

García Márquez's short stories as well as his novels depict social and religious realities of Colombia, with its still-powerful background of violence and perennial quest to find, in religious beliefs, a solution to its endless problems. García Márquez's narrative framework and settings represent the physical conditions of daily life in rural Colombia. Consequently, we find a cross-section of society including the church, the judge, the mayor, the priest, the barber, the storekeeper/owner, the families, the billiard hall, the cemetery, and a variety of women in their roles as housewives, widows, grandmothers, church servants, and prostitutes. These characters exist in a world of constant oppression, poverty, violence, diseases, unfulfilled dreams, and repetitive nightmares which mirror their feelings toward the nation's sociopolitical reality as reflected by their climate. A world of endless rains and unbearable heat where hopes for improvement or positive changes are as fleeting as the good feelings brought about by the change of seasons.

Vargas Llosa (1971) found similarities between the climatological phenomenon of intensive and endless rains with human characters' physical and spiritual lives, as well as their social environment; these characters suffer from anxiety, desolation, paralysis, and finally corruption and death. "La lluvia está infligiendo a Isabel, a su familia y a todo Macondo la misma muerte que la realidad infligió a la Aracataca de la memoria de García Márquez cuando él volvió al pueblo con su madre" (242).

In regard to the human attitude toward easily forgetting the bad times as well as the bad weather conditions once they are over, García Márquez, in *El Olor de la Guayaba*, affirms:

> La historia de América Latina es también una suma de esfuerzos desmesurados e inútiles y de dramas condenados de antemano al olvido. La peste del olvido existe también entre nosotros. Pasado el tiempo, nadie reconoce por cierta la masacre de los trabajadores de la compañía bananera, se acuerda del coronel Aureliano Buendía (104-05).

Excess of climate and the cycle of change without real modification reflect this attitude which the author implicitly generalizes to the continent as a whole.

Cultural and geographical identity, climate and aspects of daily life of his Caribbean birthplace have exerted decisive influences upon García Márquez's works, not only as faithful depictions of physical realities of the geographical setting of his stories but also as means of mirroring and externalizing characters' feelings about their personal, religious, and social lives.

Meteorological aspects of climate, especially the endless rains and the hot season, serve to represent indirectly, yet forcefully, García Márquez's impressions of the endless socio-political situation, suggesting that people's feelings of lethargy result from the apparent futility of efforts to bring about meaningful change.

García Márquez's own words quoted by Apuleyo Mendoza (1982), may best summarize his feelings about his birthplace, one of his main sources of inspiration, with all of its contrasts, contradictions, and complexity:

> Yo creo que el Caribe me enseñó a ver la realidad de otra manera, a aceptar los elementos sobrenaturales como algo que forma parte de nuestra vida cotidiana . . . . La síntesis humana y los contrastes que hay en el Caribe no se ven en otro lugar del mundo . . . . No sólo es el mundo que me enseñó a escribir, sino tambien la única región donde yo no me siento extranjero (74).

The special, peculiar flavor of this writer's fictional world results from the unique blending of sociocultural ambiance, personal feelings and recollections, and extreme and powerful climatological factors whose junction is both mimetic and symbolic.

Works Cited

Apuleyo Mendoza, Plinio, and Gabriel García Márquez. *El olor de la guayaba: Conversaciones con Plinio Apuleyo Mendoza.* Barcelona: Editorial Bruguera, 1982.

Ayala, P. Fernando. *Manual de Literatura Colombiana.* Bogotá: Educar Editores, 1984.

Benson, John. "La trampa de la nostalgia en el nuevo periodismo de García Márquez." Paper presented at MIFLC. Radford, Virginia, 12 October, 1990.

García Márquez, Gabriel. *Collected Stories*. New York: Harper and Row, Publishers, 1984.

Jansen, André. *La novela hispanoamericana actual y sus antecedentes*. Barcelona: Editorial Labor, S.A., 1973.

McNerney, Kathleen. *Understanding Gabriel García Márquez*. Columbia: University of South Carolina Press, 1989.

Martinez, S. Pedro. *Sobre García Márquez*. Montevideo: Biblioteca de Marcha, 1971.

Vargas Llosa, Mario. *García Márquez: Historia de un Deicidio*. Barcelona: Barral Editores, S. A., 1971.

Williams, L. Raymond. *Gabriel García Márquez*. Boston: Twayne Publishers, 1984.

 Creating an Atmosphere:
Depiction of Climate in the Works
of Gabriel García Márquez

Gary S. Elbow

> It rained for four years, eleven months, and two days. There were periods of drizzle during which everyone put on his full dress and a convalescent look to celebrate the clearing, but the people soon grew accustomed to interpret the pauses as a sign of redoubled rain. The sky crumbled into a set of destructive storms and out of the north came hurricanes that scattered roofs about and knocked down walls and uprooted every last plant of the banana groves.
>
> Gabriel García Márquez, *One Hundred Years of Solitude*, 291.

The Colombian novelist and Nobel Prize laureate Gabriel García Márquez has gained worldwide acclaim as an author whose writings reveal universal truths about the human condition. He is also a profoundly regional writer whose fiction is set in his homeland, the Caribbean coast of Colombia. Mario Vargas Llosa acknowledges this dualistic aspect when he refers to García Márquez's best known work, *One Hundred Years of Solitude*, as a novel that has "the unusual merit of being simultaneously traditional and modern, American and universal..." (106).[1] This paper focuses on the local and regional aspects of García Márquez's writing, specifically his depiction of climate and weather phenomena in northern Colombia.[2]

Much of the work of García Márquez reflects the author's experiences growing up in Aracataca, a small town in northern Colombia (McMurray 2). In his writing, García Márquez has transformed Aracataca into the fictional town of Macondo, made world famous as the setting of *One Hundred Years of Solitude*. Numerous critics have noted the true historical base from which *One Hundred Years of Solitude* and other works of García Márquez are derived and one student of his work even attributes to him "having created an entire human geography" (Bell-Villada 7). In addition to human geography, the works of García Márquez present a wealth of detail on vegetation, climate, weather, and other elements of physical geography. García Márquez is noted for his use of magical realism, the technique of presenting magical or physically impossible events or actions in his novels as if they were real. However, as Bell-Villada notes, he also pays great attention to detail and takes great pains to maintain "fidelity to reality itself" (107). The seeming paradox of combining magical realism with fidelity to reality is resolved by the author in several ways (Bell-Villada 109-10). Some of the fantasy borders on the plausible, and may, in fact, derive from real events. García Márquez also employs exaggeration as a vehicle for distorting the real into the magical, but almost always with specific (accurate) details or exact numbers, which give the events described a level of credibility they otherwise would lack. Finally, some events of pure fantasy are so interwoven with the context of the story that they take on a reality of their own. The key to success with all of these strategies seems to be basing them in a factual and accurate framework derived from the author's personal experience and research.

García Márquez often includes descriptions of weather and climate in his novels and short stories. Such descriptions may be incorporated into the flow of story development, as in the novella, *The Incredible and Sad Tale of Innocent Eréndira and Her Heartless Grandmother* (henceforth abbreviated to *Eréndira*). In this story, wind and aridity are agents that set mood and, in the case of the wind, determine the fate of the title character. In other works, such as *One Hundred Years of Solitude,* atmospheric conditions may set the mood of the action or, less frequently, play a role in shaping the behavior of a character.[3]

As a geographer, I am interested in analyzing the work of García Márquez in order to assess the extent to which he distorts or accurately characterizes the climatatic conditions of the settings for his work and to examine how climate and weather are used as active elements in his stories. In this paper, I will focus on three of García Márquez's works, the novel *One Hundred Years of Solitude*, the novella *Eréndira,* and the short story "Monologue of Isabel Watching it Rain in Macondo."

García Márquez writes of his *patria,* or homeland, the Caribbean lowlands of northern Colombia. Specifically, *One Hundred Years of Solitude* and "Monologue of Isabel Watching It Rain in Macondo" are set in the mythical town of Macondo, which is modeled on García Márquez's birthplace, Aracataca. *Eréndira* is set in the arid coastal zone of the western side of the Guajira Peninsula. Both of these areas are characterized by climatic anomalies. That is, they have climates that differ from what is predicted for their latitude and continental position by the standard world climate models.[4]

The Caribbean coast faces the Northeasterly Tradewinds and, according to standard models, should have a hot and humid climate. Explanations for the dryness that characterizes this area are not very satisfactory, but generally assume some process that causes atmospheric stability along the coast, preventing the air flowing in off the Caribbean Sea from rising, cooling, and causing precipitation when it comes in contact with land surfaces, as would normally be expected at this latitude.

Aracataca lies at the western base of the Sierra Nevada de Santa Marta and in the lee of the Tradewinds. Normally, such a leeside location would be as dry as the coastal areas or even drier, but this is not the case with Aracataca, which is much wetter than any of the nearby coastal areas. This anomalous pattern of precipitation is accounted for by the fact that the trade winds are held close to the surface by persistent temperature inversions along the eastern and northern flanks of the mountains (perhaps the same inversions that inhibit precipitation at the coast), so the air flows around the mountain rather than over it, bringing precipitation to the western, leeside areas.

Despite the attention that García Márquez pays to detail, it seems unlikely that he is aware of the extent to which the climate of his homeland deviates from the expected patterns developed from world climate models. However, it is important to note that the region's climate is anomalous for its latitude and orientation toward the coast. Despite this, the author presents a relatively faithful description of the weather and climate of Aracataca in his fictional accounts of Macondo and of the Guajira Peninsula in *Eréndira*. Bearing in mind the atypical climate of northern Colombia, one may infer that García Márquez's accounts reflect his own perception of these unique conditions and are not based on some generic image of what tropical climates should be like.

The Caribbean coast of South America between the Paría Peninsula in Venezuela and the approximate longitude of Cartagena, Colombia has a low annual rainfall with a dual precipitation maximum in May-June and September-November. Precipitation along the coast is generally below 500 mm (20 in.) annually, well under the amount of rainfall required to compensate for the relatively high evaporation rates. This gives much of the area a desert-like aspect, with large cacti, thorny scrub brush, and other vegetation reminiscent of drier areas such as the Sonoran Desert around Phoenix or Tucson. Rainy days are rare, probably fewer than 30 per year in the drier areas, with the number increasing toward the less arid south. The Guajira Peninsula is the most arid section of the coast. It has been described as:

> . . . a vast, hot desert covered only by low xerophilous shrubs, cacti and bromeliads. Only during the months of October and November do any rains fall and then the yellow desert is suddenly covered with various shades of green. But for the rest of the year, the

Guajira is Colombia's driest territory—a barren stretch of land surrounded by a violent sea. (Reichel-Dolmatoff, 32)

The Guajira Peninsula forms the setting for *Eréndira,* and the characteristic aridity and persistent wind of that region become, in the imagination of García Márquez, active elements, almost protagonists, in the development of the story.

Persistent winds are a distinctive feature of the climate of many coastal areas. This is especially true of windward coasts in the Tradewind belts such as the Caribbean coast of Colombia, where wind speed averages over 6.8 m/sec. (15 miles per hour) during February and only slightly less during January and March. Even in October, the least windy month, the wind averages 2.7 m/sec (6 miles per hour).[5]

The major topographic feature of Caribbean coastal Colombia is the Sierra Nevada de Santa Marta, a large mountain mass that lies southwest of the Guajira Peninsula. The Sierra Nevada de Santa Marta rises from sea level to nearly 5,800 m. (17,400 ft.) in a distance of less than 50 km. (31 mi.). On a clear day, its snow-capped peaks can be seen from the city of Santa Marta and other coastal locations.

Aracataca lies at the western base of the Sierra, in an area that receives an average annual rainfall of 1,600 mm. (64 in), or nearly four times the annual precipitation of the adjacent coastal zones. The number of days with rain per year is probably in excess of 100. This amount of precipitation is sufficient to give the area a humid tropical climate. However, even in Aracataca there is a pronounced annual dry season that lasts from November through April, with January, February, and March generally receiving no precipitation at all.

It is this unexpectedly high precipitation, along with the availability of irrigation water in streams draining from the Sierra, that made the area around Aracataca suitable for banana production and which, in turn, attracted the United Fruit Company to establish plantations there around the turn of this century. When one realizes how atypical his birthplace is of the rest of the eastern Caribbean coast of Colombia, it is easy to understand the preoccupation that García Márquez shows with precipitation and, especially, with the prolonged rainy periods that figure so prominently in *One Hundred Years of Solitude* and "Monologue of Isabel Watching the Rain in Macondo."

Eréndira, first published in 1972, and made into a film in 1984, presents some prime examples of the ways in which the author uses weather and climate in his work. The story features two key climatic elements, wind and aridity. The "wind of misfortune" causes the fire that destroys the house of Eréndira's grandmother, and it is the same wind that presages Eréndira's unsuccessful attempt to flee with her lover, Ulises, and that causes the death of the mysterious photographer. In the last lines of the story, it is the wind into which Eréndira flees when she disappears into the desert. García Márquez gives us a sense of the impact of the wind on the psyche with the lines:

> There was a cistern in the courtyard for the storage of water carried over many years from distant springs on the backs of Indians, and hitched to a ring on the cistern wall was a broken-down ostrich, the only feathered creature who could survive the torment of that accursed climate. The house was far away from everything, in the heart of the desert, next to a settlement with miserable and burning streets where the goats committed suicide from desolation when the wind of misfortune blew. (3)

In the wind swept Great Plains of the United States, old-timers talk of the psychological impact of persistent and strong winds on pioneer women living in isolated houses on the plains. The wind seemed to deepen the women's sense of loneliness, isolation, and hopelessness of eking out a living from the barren plain.[6] García Márquez seems to suggest a similar response in his references to the wind of misfortune. No doubt, he had experienced the persistent winds of the Caribbean coast, and had gained a feeling for the sense of desolation and desperation brought on by the constant whistling of the wind around the walls of houses and across the uneven ground. García Márquez strengthens this sense and adds to the magical quality of the account by giving the wind a consciousness: ". . . the wind went around the house looking for a way in" (5), and "A short while later the wind of her misfortune came into the bedroom like a pack of hounds and knocked the candle over against the curtain" (7). Thus, García Márquez takes an element of the existing climate and incorporates it into the story, giving it the role of a collaborator or an active participant in the flow of the narrative.

In a similar vein, García Márquez makes frequent references to the desert. In this case he seems to exaggerate the true nature of the Caribbean coast, suggesting heat and barrenness far greater than what exist in reality. One can imagine that this exaggerated image of barrenness and desolation is derived, at least in part, from the contrast with the fecundity of the more humid slopes of the Sierra Nevada de Santa Marta and, especially, with Aracataca. In any case, "Eréndira" is replete with references to aridity, heat, dust, desolation, and words designed to evoke an image of the desert. The exaggeration of these images is typical of García Márquez's employment of magical realism and, in this case, they provide a suitable backdrop for highlighting the barrenness and desolation of Eréndira's life. Thus, the portrayal of a harsh and barren natural landscape emphasizes the depth of Eréndira's human tragedy.

The setting of Eréndira's deflowering during a rainstorm provides a stark contrast with the normally arid desert. Perhaps García Márquez is trying to relate the violence of the storm to the violence with which Eréndira is forced to surrender her virginity; or perhaps the rain symbolizes the fate that awaits Eréndira as she faces a dismal and seemingly hopeless future. Whatever the purpose of the rainstorm, its characterization seems to parallel, on a smaller scale, the much better developed and more characteristic accounts of rainstorms that appear in *One Hundred Years of Solitude* and "Monologue of Isabel Watching It Rain in Macondo."

In the "Monologue of Isabel," from the collection *Leafstorm and Other Stories,* rain dominates the action of the story. As the title suggests, the entire tale is a first-person narrative of a woman who recounts her changing moods during a six-day rainstorm. The story opens with the line: "Winter fell one Sunday when people were coming out of church." Two lines farther into the story we learn that winter begins in May and, still farther on, that "summer" lasts for seven months (197-8). Winter in the Hispanic tropics refers to the rainy season, and summer to the dry season, a carry-over from the Mediterranean climate of Iberia, which is characterized by dry summers and rainy winters. This account of the climate of the fictional Macondo matches almost perfectly the seasonality of climate for Caribbean Colombia that was noted earlier in this essay. This is a prime example of the author's attention to accurate detail. The onset of the tropical rainy seasons is often very abrupt, beginning with a violent rainstorm that follows months of near total aridity. This characteristic of tropical climates is well portrayed in the story of Isabel.

As for the remainder of the account, in which García Márquez has his narrator describe the six days of continuous heavy rain, accompanied by floods that kill cattle and float corpses out of their graves, to what extent has the author's imagination exaggerated reality? Unless one actually lives in Aracataca for a period of years, or possesses detailed climate records, it is impossible to provide a definitive answer to this question.[7] Still, on the basis of the information that is available, we may be able to draw some inferences. We know, for example, that Aracataca receives about 1600 mm. (64 in.) of rainfall during the year and that it is concentrated in the period May-October. Since the remaining months of the year are largely dry, this means that it must rain on nearly a daily basis during the wetter parts of the rainy season. Of course, the normal daily precipitation pattern of the tropics would call for afternoon thundershowers of relatively short duration, followed by clearing. However, occasional tropical disturbances called easterly waves pass over the low latitude tropics, bringing with them periods of persistent rain that may last for several days. On rare occasions, as with Hurricane Joan in 1988, these disturbances develop into full-blown tropical cyclones that are capable of causing considerable flooding and wind damage. While it seems unlikely that an easterly wave would often generate continuous rains of six-days' duration, three or four days is probably fairly common, especially if two disturbances happen to come close together, and the occurrence of a longer period of steady precipitation does seem to fall well within the range of probability. All of this suggests that García Márquez's representation of climate in "Monologue of Isabel Watching It Rain in Macondo" is a rather faithful depiction of reality.

If García Márquez's characterization of the climate in Isabel's monologue approximates reality, his well-known account of a prolonged rain storm in *One Hundred Years of Solitude,* the opening lines of which are printed at the beginning of this paper, more than compensates as an example of magical realism. Of course, this infamous rain, which lasts for four years, eleven months, and two days, and is followed by a ten year drought, appears to violate all of the norms of the real climate of Aracataca, or any other place on earth, for that matter. This is magical realism at its best and most outrageous. However, when this incident is placed within its context in the novel, it begins to make some sense. The endless rain follows on the heels of government denials that 3,000 striking banana workers were killed by the army. This denial is a form of official magical realism that was urged by Mr. Brown, the North American director of the banana company that has its plantations in Macondo. If the government can invent fiction at Mr. Brown's behest and substitute it for reality, then even the rules of nature are vulnerable. Thus, García Márquez can imagine the same Mr. Brown to be capable of altering the natural rainy and dry season cycles that are characteristic of Macondo. Interpreted in this manner, the account of almost five years of steady rain followed by a ten year drought seems to be a clear attempt to parallel through a violation of the rules of nature the government's ability to deny the massacre witnessed by José Arcadio Buendía.[8] But, even in this distortion, the fundamental pattern of rainy season followed by dry is maintained, and it is also a prime example of the author's use of precise, if imaginary, numbers to add versimilitude to his magical accounts.

Critics have noted the circularity of the narrative in *One Hundred Years of Solitude* (Carreras González 49-51; Siemans 360). Circularity is expressed in repeating names of the male line of Buendías and in events depicted in the book. This circularity is paralleled in the repeating annual patterns of precipitation that characterize the climate of Macondo. One could argue that the distortion of these patterns toward the end of the saga reflects the inevitable progress toward extinction of the Buendías. Just as the account of climate defies the repeating norms that have been established longer than memory, so does the Buendía family finally break a pattern that has persisted for a century as it nears its demise.

García Márquez demonstrates clearly in his writing that he has carefully observed the patterns of weather and climate of his *patria*. He sometimes records these patterns with considerable faithfulness, as is demonstrated in "Monologue of Isabel Watching it Rain in Macondo." And, when the writer does deviate from reality, it seems to be intentional and for the purpose of achieving a specific effect. This conclusion is exemplified in the case of the distortion of natural rainy/dry cycles in *One Hundred Years of Solitude*. So, one may conclude that, with regard to depiction of weather and climate, García Márquez's reality becomes magical when it suits his purposes, but that his work may approach realism far more closely than many readers, looking for the magic in his writings, may expect.

Notes

1. Rendered in the original Spanish as: "...*esta novela que tiene el mérito poco común de ser, simultáneamente, tradicional y moderna, americana y universal* . . . ." Gene Bell-Villada echoes this point in his recent book, *García Márquez: The Man and His Work,* with the comment that *Cien Años de Soledad* can be seen "as a metaphor for the rise and decline of all human civilizations . . ." (116).

2. Weather is generally defined by meteorologists as the conditions of the atmosphere at a particular time and location. Climate refers to the conditions that would normally be expected to occur at some location during a specific time of year. The weather on any given day may or may not be consistent with the established patterns of climate.

3. The use of climate, especially the symbolism of heat, in the writings of García Márquez is discussed in Volkenning and Carreras González.

4. Descriptions of the climates of northern Colombia are taken from Trewartha, 57 *et passim* and Snow, 295-403.

5. For comparative purposes, normal average wind speeds for Lubbock, Texas, generally considered to be a relatively windy site, are: windiest months (March and April) 14.8 mph, the least windy month (August) 10.0 mph, and the annual average, 12.5 mph (National Oceanic and Atmospheric Administration n.d., 3).

6. The psychological role of wind in the Plains is dramatically presented in Dorothy Scarborough's novel *The Wind,* and the Lillian Gish silent film of the same name, which is an account of the effect of wind on a young woman who moved from Virginia to West Texas in the late 1900s.

7. A Colombian acquaintance from Barranquilla has related to me that she has experienced rainy periods of up to four days and that the resulting floods bring with them down the barrancas an astounding assortment of flotsam, including occasional corpses.

8. The true history behind the account of the banana worker massacre is discussed at length in Bell-Villada's "Banana Strike and Military Massacre: *One Hundred Years of Solitude* and What Happened in 1928."

Works Cited

Bell-Villada, Gene H. "Banana Strike and Military Massacre: *One Hundred Years of Solitude* and What Happened in 1928." *From Dante to García Márquez: Studies in Romance Literatures and Linguistics,* Ed. by Gene H. Bell-Villada, Antonio Giménez, and George Pistorius. Williamstown, Mass.: Williams College, 1987.

———. *García Márquez: The Man and His Work.* Chapel Hill, NC: University of North Carolina Press, 1990.

Carreras González, Olga. *El mundo de Macondo en la Obra de Gabriel García Márquez.* Miami: Ediciones Universal, 1974.

García Márquez, Gabriel. *One Hundred Years of Solitude.* Trans. Gregory Rabassa. New York: Avon, 1970.

———. "Monologue of Isabel Watching It Rain in Macondo." *Leaf Storm and Other Stories.* Trans. Gregory Rabassa. New York: Avon, 1972.

———. "The Incredible and Sad Tale of Eréndira and Her Heartless Grandmother." *Innocent Eréndira and Other Stories by Gabriel García Márquez.* Trans. Gregory Rabassa. New York: Harper & Row, 1978.

George R. McMurray. *Gabriel García Márquez.* New York: Frederick Ungar, 1977.

National Oceanic and Atmospheric Administration, United States Department of Commerce. *Local Climatological Data: 1990 Annual Summary with Comparative Data, Lubbock, Texas.* National Oceanic and Atmospheric Administration, National Climatic Data Center: Nashville, North Carolina, n.d.

Reichel-Dolmatoff, Gerardo. *Colombia.* New York: Praeger, 1965.

Scarborough, Dorothy. *The Wind.* 1925. Austin: University of Texas Press, 1979.

Siemans, William L. "Tiempo, entropía y la estructura de *Cien Años de Soledad.*" *Explicación de Cien Años de Soledad.* San José, Costa Rica: Porrata y Avendaño, 1976.

Snow, J. W. "The Climate of Northern South America." *Climates of Central and South America.* Ed. Werner Schwerdtfeger. Amsterdam: Elsevier, 1976.

Trewartha, Glenn T. *The Earth's Problem Climates.* Madison: University of Wisconsin Press, 1961.

Vargas Llosa, Mario. "El Amadís en America." *Sobre García Márquez.* Ed. Pedro Simón Mártinez. Montevideo: Biblioteca de Marcha, 1971.

Volkening, Ernesto. "Gabriel García Márquez o el Trópico Desembrujado," *Eco* 7 (agosto 1963): 275-93. Rpt. in *9 Asedios a García Márquez.* Ed. Mario Benedetti. Santiago: Editorial Universitaria, 1969.

The Weather as a Story Element in Four Short Works from Latin America

Paul Nelson

The use of the weather as a story element is nothing new to literature, because the weather forms such a part of man's life. It can alter his moods, and he often attributes to it his triumphs and failures. Writers have used the weather in their works for centuries to reflect the optimism, pessimism, and doubt they themselves feel, and have used the weather to heighten the emotion of their works as well.

As a literary element, the weather can be manipulated just as a character, in order to heighten or underscore what is going on in the work. This usage was particularly popular among English poets prior to 1856, when John Ruskin coined the term "pathetic fallacy" to describe the projection of human emotions onto nature. As a literary element, the use of weather—one aspect of nature—falls under this heading. Ruskin, however, used the term pejoratively to describe the overuse of nature personified in the English poets of his day (161-77). In the case of four twentieth century Latin American prose writers—Hernando Téllez, Gabriel García Márquez, Enrique Jaramillo Levi, and Baldomero Lillo, the "pathetic fallacy" in the form of the inclusion of the weather as a story element is not used sentimentally as Ruskin described. Instead, the weather as a story element is used in a skillful and artistic manner to draw attention to the oppressive situations in which the characters find themselves.

Hernando Téllez, a Colombian writer overshadowed today by fellow countryman Gabriel García Márquez, is perhaps better known as an essayist than as a short story writer. However, his collection of short stories, *Cenizas para el viento y otras historias*, published in 1950, has earned him a position of prestige among Latin American writers. Téllez broke with the "costumbrista" tradition of his predecessors, who represented Colombia as an idyllic, peaceful country, and instead presents in his stories an image of an anguished and bloody country—a bitter yet realistic picture of his homeland.

In his most anthologized story "Espuma y nada más," a strong sense of weather permeates the work. The "heat" is commented on directly twice and once indirectly. These comments may at first appear to be very few, but, in a "short" short story such as this, each detail receives much more weight than in longer narratives. In much the way that the impressionist painter uses tiny brush strokes to create a total picture, Téllez's impressionistic-like descriptions of the weather present very clearly a torrid climate—hot and volatile. In "Espuma y nada más," a barber, who is a revolutionary at heart, must shave the man responsible for the execution of his fellow revolutionaries. The barber is confronted with a moral dilemma: slit the captain's throat or shave him as his "oficio" requires, since the barber is, after all, a professional who must perform his duty.

The "heat," as mentioned, is commented on only three times in this story—at the beginning, in the middle, and at the end. The captain is the first to mention it, saying: "Hace un calor de todos los demonios" (19).

Toward the middle of the work, it is the barber who comments on it in an interior monologue: "¡Qué calor! Torres [the captain] debe estar sudando como yo" (21).

The third mention comes at the story's end, when the barber comments that he is "soaking wet" with perspiration, describing indirectly the heat in the barber shop.

The description of the weather in Téllez's story reflects an oppressive situation; the people's discontent with their government has led them to take "revolutionary" actions. The government in turn "stamps out" those responsible for these actions. Furthermore, the pressure of the barber's rather uncomfortable predicament is emphasized by the sense of the heat. His reaction to this stressful situation is perfectly "real," since the human body does react to stressful situations with an increase in body temperature and the phenomenon of perspiring, a phenomenon that gives rise to such expressions in English as "the heat is on." The mention of the heat in Téllez's story, however, does more than merely characterize the barber in his predicament or contribute to the story's tropical setting. Its oppressiveness underscores the atmosphere of oppression in Colombia that Téllez wishes to depict in his story.

Gabriel García Márquez, although overshadowing Téllez today, follows his fellow Colombian's lead in his much anthologized short short story "Un día de estos."[2] In this story, a picture of Colombia's society similar to that of Téllez's is presented. In fact, Márquez's story is very reminiscent of Téllez's "Espuma y nada más" and seems almost to be a response to it. A similar situation is presented, but a different climax is reached. Téllez's story is constructed around the narrator's inner conflict and is narrated as an internal monologue. Márquez's story, on the other hand, is told through a third person, self-effacing narrator in a style similar to Hemingway's, the result being a story told mainly through implication.

In "Un día de éstos," a dentist with beliefs contrary to the ruling government's is obliged to take care of the mayor's abscessed tooth. The dentist refuses to do so at first, but relents when the mayor threatens to shoot him. The dentist, however, has the upper hand of this situation and extracts more than just the mayor's tooth. By telling the mayor he cannot use any anesthetic, he "extracts" a "mental" and a somewhat sadistic physical revenge on his patient. The tables are turned and the oppressed becomes the oppressor; the dentist sets things right... but only for a brief moment: "Aquí nos paga veinte muertos, teniente," says the dentist calmly upon pulling the mayor's tooth. This statement fills us in on what has been going on. It is a picture of Colombian society similar to Téllez's—an oppressed people at the mercy of an oppressive government.

Like Téllez, Márquez also includes the weather in his story, but in a way inverse to Téllez's use. The climactic tooth extraction, a gesture of revenge, is prefigured in Márquez's descriptive first sentence: "El lunes amaneció tibio y sin lluvia" (23). In the third paragraph, two turkey buzzards are drying themselves in the sun, and the dentist "siguió trabajando con la idea de que antes del almuerzo volvería a llover" (23).

After extracting the mayor's tooth, near the story's end, the narrator says that the dentist "vio el cielo raso desfondado."

The weather here is used to reflect the outlook of the dentist. Things could have gone badly, but they didn't, and nature confirms that the dentist has done the right thing by showing a clear sky with no threat of rain. Márquez's use of projecting human emotions on nature falls perfectly into Ruskin's description of the "pathetic fallacy," yet Márquez uses it artfully, avoiding any resultant sentimentality.

It is interesting to note the description of the mayor after the operation: "Inclinado sobre la escupidera, sudoroso, jadeante, se desabotonó la guerrera ..." (25-26).

Although the weather doesn't enter here precisely, the mention of the mayor's perspiring brings the element of heat into the story. The mayor has felt a certain form of oppression at the hands of someone with a certain power. Márquez, as mentioned above, succeeds in inverting Téllez's story with the result that the oppressed becomes the oppressor.

Another kind of oppressive situation appears in Panamenian Enrique Jaramillo Levi's short short story "El cortejo."[3] In this story, the element of weather, also the heat, underscores an oppressive personal relationship—one of husband and wife.

A contemporary writer who is not very well known yet, Jaramillo Levi has written poetry and drama as well as fiction. His story "El cortejo" appears in his collection of stories titled *El buho que dejó de latir,* published in 1974. Jaramillio Levi, in the words of Enrique Anderson Imbert, "[es] el cuentista con una conciencia del oficio más educada y una obra más sostenida.... No se disimula su voluntad experimentadora" (408). Jaramillo Levi's talent has not gone unnoticed, however. In 1971, he was awarded the "Beca Centroamericana de Literatura" by the "Centro Mexicano de Ecritores." Furthermore, his collection of stories *El buho que dejó de latir* received honorable mention in the "Tercer Certamen Cultural Centroamericano." Jaramillo Levi currently resides in Panamá, where he is professor at the Universidad de Panamá and director of the magazine *Maga,* of which he is also the founder.

In "El cortejo," the heat of a Panamenian village permeates the story. A man leaves his house at midday and tails along after a passing funeral procession, noticing that the intense noon heat bothers him less and less. Later he realizes that the funeral procession he has been following is carrying his cadaver to the graveyard . . . and that it was his wife who has killed him.

The descriptions of the heat in Jaramillo Levi's story create a stifling effect—matching the stifled relationship the man has had with his wife. The first mention of the heat comes when the narrator describes the village the man now lives in as "un pueblito caluroso" (91). The man moved there because of his wife, but now regrets having left his home city of Colón: "En días como hoy, cuando de la tierra reseca parecía brotar un vaho opresivo que le mordía la planta de los pies con saña, suspiraba pensando en las playas que bañaban su ciudad" (91).

Jaramillo Levi's use of the heat as a story element serves two functions: (1) The man's noting that the heat bothers him less and less foreshadows his shocking realization at the story's end; (2) the man's escape from the heat parallels his "escape" from his oppressive home situation. Jaramillo Levi, then, follows in his colleagues' footsteps, using the weather as a story element in much the same way that Téllez and Márquez have. Its inclusion in his story parallels and underscores the oppressive relationship found in the work.

In these three "short" short stories, the aspect of weather used to underscore the oppressive situations is the heat. In another Latin American writer's work, Baldomero Lillo's "El pago,"[4] the rain and the cold are used to underscore the oppressive situation that the characters find themselves in. Lillo's use of the cold reflects the climate of his homeland of Chile, as opposed to the hot climates of Colombia and Panama.

Lillo, usually associated with the Naturalist movement near the end of the last century, uses the element of weather extensively in his story "El pago," which appears in his collection of short stories, *Sub Terra* (1904). This collection of stories, inspired by Emile Zola's *Germinal,* describes the abuse of Chile's coal miners at the hands of the big mining companies.

In "El Pago," Pedro María, an almost-over-the-hill thirty-five-year-old miner with a wife and two young children at home, works laboriously in the mines. The next day, payday, he hopes to receive enough money in wages to buy back the household items that they have put into hock in order to eat. Pedro and his wife wait in line to be paid, but his name is not called. His pay has been retained in retribution for having broken holes in the mineshaft's walls.

The use of the weather in this short story is much more extensive than in the previous three stories. Lillo uses the cold, windy, and rainy weather of the Chilean winter to foreshadow Pedro María's fate, as well as to symbolize the mining company's oppression. When Pedro María left the mine to return home, "las corrientes de aire que encontraba al paso habían enfriado su cuerpo" (49-50).

Outside the mine "un soplo helado le azotó el rostro . . . . Sobre su cabeza grandes masas de nubes oscuras corrían empujadas por un fuerte viento del septentrián" (50).

The weather up to this point does not appear very promising, although there are still some signs of optimism for what is to transpire on payday: "El plateado disco de la luna lanzado en dirección contraria, parecía penetrar con la violencia de un proyectil, palideciendo y eclipsándose entre los densos nubarrones para reaparecer de nuevo, rápido y brillante" (50).

The night before payday, as Pedro María rests comfortably on his primitive cot, all is silent in his shack, except for the gusts of wind and rain that assault the shack's outside walls. Payday arrives, and Lillo's description of the weather presages Pedro María's fate: "Una llovizna fina y persistente caía del cielo entoldado, de un gris oscuro y ceniciento. Por el lado del mar una espesa cortina de brumas cerraba el horizonte, como un muro opaco que avanzaba lentamente tragándose a su paso todo lo que la vista percibía en aquella dirección" (51). The image of the opaque "wall" of rain closing in and slowly "swallowing up" the horizon is symbolic of the mining company's oppression of its workers—it "swallows up" all of their hopes. Pedro María's destiny, as prefigured in this description of the weather, is ill-fated.

At the story's end, the rain becomes a symbol of the pervasive oppressiveness of the mining company: "La lluvia caía siempre, copiosa, incesante empapando la tierra" (58).

Without getting paid, Pedro María cannot even buy firewood to warm his house so that the cold enters. The oppression of the mining company is absolute. Broke, humiliated, and utterly downtrodden by the company, Pedro María can do nothing but find a dry spot of earth and sleep. So weak is he in mind and spirit that he succumbs to the oppression. When he awakens, it is still raining—the company is triumphant: "Las gotas de lluvia modulaban aún su alegre sinfonía, escurrinédose rápidas por el alero de los tejados" (60).

Lillo's use of the weather as a story element can also be classified as the "pathetic fallacy," since human emotion is seen projected in it. Lillo's use of this "fallacy," however, is an ironic one, for rather than sympathizing with the story's protagonist, the weather seems to sympathize with the mining company and delights in Pedro María's situation. Such usage creates a great sense of pathos for this character, which was, after all, Lillo's main goal in *Sub Terra*.

In conclusion, two generalizations emerge concerning the use of the weather as a story element in the works of the above four Latin American writers. First, the inclusion of the weather, whether hot or cold, is used to accentuate the tone of oppression the authors create in the stories, and the weather underscores the oppressive circumstances the characters find themselves in. Second, the "pathetic fallacy" is alive and well in Latin America. Although not found in the works of Téllez and Jaramillo Levi per se, the pathetic fallacy is most definitely found in the works of Márquez and Lillo, where it is an artistic manifestation, and not the "fallacy" that Ruskin describes.

Works Cited

Anderson Imbert, Enrique. *Historia de la literatura hispanoamericana*. 2nd ed. 2 vols. México: Fondo de Cultura Económica. 1970. Vol 2.
García Márquez, Gabriel. *Los funerales de la Mamá Grande*. 1962. Buenos Aires: Editorial Sudamericana, 1976.
Jaramillo Levi, Enrique. *El buho que dejó de latir*. México: Samo, 1974.
Lillo, Baldomero. *Sub Terra*. 1904. Santiago: Nascimento, 1966.
Ruskin, John. *Modern Painters*. 1856. 3rd ed. 6 vols. London, 1898-1091. Vol 3.
Téllez, Hernando. *Cenizas para el viento y otras historias*. 1950. Santiago, Chile: Universitaria, 1969.

 Heat, Water, and Stars in *Pedro Páramo*

Cida S. Chase

Anyone who has read Juan Rulfo's *Pedro Páramo* has discovered that this work is an intricate pluralistic novel replete with mysteries and uncertainties. From the beginning, the reader comes in touch with a landscape which appears to be vanishing because the seemingly perpendicular rays of the August sun turn the plain into a mirage. This vision of reverberating desert does not become fully meaningful until the reader has absorbed the full text and understands the landscape's intimate relationship with the sterile and empty spiritual essence of the characters.

Moreover, the reader meets a narrator who remains unidentified for a lengthy part of the narrative and suddenly, violating most traditions of narrativity, turns out to be dead. Soon one encounters a proliferation of narrative voices; some are identifiable but others are not. These voices, which produce multiple points of view, represent characters who do not act surprised at all at the strange happenings in Comala. Since time is liberated from the usual human perspective, the chronology is dislocated and the structural patterns of the novel seem to follow the lines of an abstract geometrical painting.

The fragmentary nature of this novel's structure has often caught the attention of critics who try to arrange and disarrange the segments, assigning them numbers in an effort to decipher some of the textual clues (Rulfo, 1988, 21-32). In the opinion of some readers "the fragments float as 'in the air,' between life and death, or between the before and the after, where the effects precede and persist beyond the causes, where the characters are locked in themselves as if they were in a grave and communicate with each other through monologues or through uncooperative dialogues, full of silent moments, full of equivocal absurdities"[1] (Volek 40).

However, not all the aspects of *Pedro Páramo* are elusive and slippery. Juan Rulfo has endowed his masterpiece with explicit references to climate, which may assist the reader in clearing up some of the mysteries and in recognizing the origin of some of the utterances. Moreover, Rulfo abandons his orality in the passages that contain allusions to climate. His narrative discourse becomes more suggestive, diaphanous and lyrical, soothing the reader and relieving the tension created by the text. In fact, the cadence of the passages dealing with climate serves as an escape valve from the inconclusive sobriety of the dialogues which constantly appeal to what is implied in them. The reader can thus stop worrying for a moment about questions and answers which do not coincide and enjoy a spontaneous pleasure of the text, for these passages are only comparable in lyricism to the intermittent reminiscences of Dolores Preciado about the Comala of her youth.

Climatological allusions begin very early in the novel. The reader hears Juan Preciado complain about the heat in his newly-established dialogue with the muleteer, Abundio. The latter's response is alarming and ominous. He says:

> Ya lo sentirá más fuerte cuando lleguemos a Comala.
> Aquello está sobre las brasas de la tierra, en
> la mera boca del infierno. Con decirle que muchos
> de los que allí mueren, al llegar al infierno
> regresan por su cobija (Rulfo, 1988, 68).

Comala is thus a place where the temperature reaches higher levels than hell itself. As Abundio explains, the inhabitants from Comala who die and are damned to eternal fire, find hell cooler than Comala; they come home to get their blankets and be more comfortable. The comparison between Comala and hell at the onset of the narrative provides the reader with a most effective clue as to the nature of the place for which Juan Preciado is looking. It is, in effect, a location not of this world; it belongs beyond the grave, for it is an eerie kingdom of the damned. Its inhabitants are nothing but disintegrating, whispering shadows.

It is interesting to note Rulfo's wisdom in appropriating the popular semantic content of the term Comala in his conception of a town by that name and a place which is extremely hot, sitting on the coals by hell's entrance. The term "Comala" brings to the mind of the reader the word "comal," which identifies the heavy Mexican skillet where one cooks tortillas and other native Mexican foods.[2] A "comal" sitting on a fire becomes a deadly threat to any unsuspecting soul who tries to touch it. Rulfo had discovered the optimum semantic value of the word "comal" before the publication of the first edition of *Pedro Páramo* in 1955, for he already uses it in "Nos han dado la tierra," which is included as the second short narrative in *El llano en llamas* (1953). In this story he describes the worthless land that the government awarded the peasants after the Mexican Revolution as a "comal acalorado," a heated comal (Rulfo, 1953, 18).

In addition to being an unbearably hot place, Comala has other environmental characteristics. It is a place where the atmosphere is rarefied. One can surmise that the excessive heat makes most of the air rise, making normal breathing difficult for the visitor from Sayula, Juan Preciado. This aspect begins to manifest itself even before Juan Preciado arrives in Comala. As he and Abundio come closer to Comala, Juan Preciado notices the change in the air. He comments: "Habíamos dejado el aire caliente allá arriba y nos íbamos hundiendo en el puro calor sin aire" (Rulfo 68). As he muses that they are sinking into airless heat, one understands that the air is gradually becoming more rarefied. Upon reaching Comala he notices the endless silence and points out the thinness of the air when he says that "el aire era escaso" (71). These strange atmospheric conditions allow him to hear better the voices in his mind, especially his mother's melodic voice reminiscing about the Comala of the past.

The emphasis on the lack of air, which becomes a constant trait in regard to Comala, reinforces the notion of time being static in the town. Moreover, it seems to point at one of the mysteries of the novel, the real cause of death of Juan Preciado. The reader receives two messages with respect to this issue. One possibility is that the character died of terror and the other one is that he perished from suffocation by the heat.

In regard to the terror theory, one knows that after having been in the house of the incestuous siblings, Donis and his sister, Juan Preciado's fear seems to mount to catastrophic proportions. In fact, he is the only character in the book who is frightened by the odd happenings in Comala. The other narrative voices show no surprise at all and furthermore, they do not seem to experience the need to explain these events. One can recall, for example, the matter-of-fact tone that the incestuous sister uses to tell Juan Preciado that "Aquí esas horas están llenas de espantos. Si usted viera," says she calmly "el gentío de ánimas que andan sueltas por la calle. En cuanto oscurece comienzan a salir" (119). She and the other characters speak of the wandering souls of the dead as if they were talking about the weather, while Juan Preciado, the visitor, constantly experiences fear and bewilderment, hence his tomb companion, Dorotea or Doroteo (gender seems to be of no importance in the realm of death) claims that she found him dead of fear. "Es cierto, Dorotea," agrees Preciado, "Me mataron los murmullos" (127), the whispers killed me.

Interestingly enough, this terror theory seems to have a corollary which suggests that the greatest terror that Juan Preciado experiences has more to do with his finding out what kind of person his progenitor was than with the wandering souls that he progressively finds in Comala. At the end of his self-recognition journey from Sayula to Comala, looking for his father, Juan Preciado learns and corroborates that Pedro Páramo was truly, as Abundio had told him, "un rencor vivo" (68), a living rancor. Presumably the shocking revelation about his origin and about the evil heritage that he carries within kills him (Cobo Borda, 1985, 38).

As for the suffocation theory, there is even more evidence because of the recurrent image of the lack of air in Comala. Juan Preciado initially blames his death on not being able to breathe. His feelings of suffocation become critical when he flees the house of incest in search of air. He explains his final discomfort in the following manner:

> Y es que no había aire; sólo la noche entorpecida
> y quieta, acalorada por la canícula de agosto.
> No había aire. Tuve que sorber el mismo aire
> que salía de mi boca, deteniéndolo con las manos
> antes de que se fuera. Lo sentía ir y venir, cada
> vez menos; hasta que se hizo tan delgado que
> se filtró entre mis dedos para siempre.
> Digo para siempre. (125)

As Juan Preciado firmly reiterates the idea of the lack of air and his struggle to hold on to the small amount of air that he had in his mouth, the reader can assume that the oppressive atmospheric conditions in Comala constitute an important contributing factor to the character's demise.

In addition to symbolizing the infernal deeds of the inhabitants of Comala, the concept of heat in the narrative appears associated also with a very specific kind of evil on the part of Pedro Páramo, his uncontrollable lust. One can observe this point in the fragment where Damiana Cisneros, the head maid of the Media Luna ranch, recalls the night in which Pedro Páramo invaded young Margarita's quarters. The reader can detect the intruder's unbridled bodily desires in Damiana's comment that Pedro Páramo is an incorrigible alley cat. "Ah, qué don Pedro! . . . No se le quita lo gatero" (175), says she in a joking tone. However, the idea of bestial sexual behavior is reinforced with the bellowing of the bulls that startle Damiana. The night then becomes so uncomfortably warm that Damiana must remove her night gown and when she decides to take another peek at the window, a narrator says: "le parecio que la tierra estaba llena de hervores, como cuando ha llovido y se enchina de gusanos. Sentía que se levantaba algo así como el calor de muchos hombres" (176). Lust is thus related to heat, humidity, body heat and the proliferation of earthworms.

In counterpoint with the extreme heat of Comala and other allusions to heat, the novel emphasizes the presence of water. To some readers the allusion to water is nothing but another nuisance, another aggravating element in the unbearable weather of Comala, which is possibly excessively humid. Sergio Fernández comments on this point in the following manner:

> the canicular, dog days of summer bark at space
> a symbol, perhaps, of the tortured souls of Purgatory,
> but they clash with a permanent rain, which is sometimes
> a storm, sometimes a downpour or a heavy breeze,
> or drops that slip down the eaves tediously;
> it is a rain that makes the trip, along with the heat,
> something overwhelming, exhausting. . .
> even for a dead person. (959)

However, rather than being an oppressive factor, the frequent allusions to water seem to point out happier memories of the more remote past. In fact, in addition to leading the dead into the process of reminiscing and promoting their discourse, water in the form of rain and humidity is associated with the presence of definite characters in the novel such as the adolescent Pedro Páramo.

The initial allusion to water in the form of rain occurs in relation to the temporal segments associated with Pedro Páramo's youth. The young man has sought refuge in a private place to think and to engage in his unending monologue about Susana San Juan. This segment, which is one of the most lyrical expressions of nature in the text, begins as follows:

> El agua goteaba de las tejas hacia un agujero en
> la arena del patio. Sonaba: plas plas y luego
> otra vez plas, en mitad de una hoja de laurel
> que daba vueltas y rebotes metida en la hendidura
> de los ladrillos. Ya se había ido la tormenta.
> Ahora de vez en cuando la brisa sacudía las ramas
> del granado haciéndolas chorrear una lluvia espesa,
> estampando la tierra con gotas brillantes que
> luego se empañaban. Las gallinas, engarruñadas
> como si durmieran, sacudían de pronto sus alas
> y salían al patio, picoteando de prisa, atrapando
> las lombrices desenterradas por la lluvia. Al correrse
> las nubes, el sol sacaba luz a las piedras, irisaba
> todo de colores, se bebía el agua de la tierra, jugaba
> con el aire dándole brillo a las hojas con que
> jugaba el aire. (75)

The drops of rain, the breeze playing in the plants illuminated by the recent sun, awaken activity in the backyard, and the chickens come out of their somnolence to peck the ground looking for worms. Such a lively environment brings Pedro Páramo into a self-absorbed state of mind which culminates in the image of Susana San Juan. He then remembers more joyful times and to his mind come visions of green hills, "las lomas verdes" (75), upon which he and Susana would fly a kite and watch it swirl and swing through the air like a paper bird (75-76).

When night falls Pedro Páramo resumes his monologue in his room, while somewhere in the house the women are saying the rosary. The allusions to rain return, announcing the presence of this character and his thoughts. His monologue becomes excessively sentimental as he looks at the raindrops illuminated by lightning; he sighs repeatedly and thinks of Susana: "Miraba caer las gotas iluminadas por los relámpagos, y cada vez que respiraba suspiraba, y cada vez que pensaba, pensaba en ti, Susana" (79). Nevertheless, the presence of water associated with Pedro Páramo's youth is not always a good omen. The segment that recalls the violent death of his father begins with the allusion to water dripping from a faucet or a water filter. The sound of the falling drops merges with the rumor of hasty steps shuffling along the ground. It is then that Pedro Páramo's mother, removing his blanket, wakes him up and makes the ominous announcement, "Han matado a tu padre" (89). They have murdered your father. This lugubrious memory probably emerges when Pedro Páramo, the adult, must confront the accidental death of the only other human being he ever loved besides Susana San Juan, Miguel Páramo. Miguel is the only illegitimate son he ever acknowledges, despite the novel's implication that he had fathered a legion of offspring. The death of Miguel Páramo prompts him to display an unusual facet of himself, that of a loving, devastated father who begs Padre Rentería to forgive his son's multiple trespasses (91).

The image of water in the form of rain also appears associated with Susana San Juan, when she becomes part of Pedro Páramo's adult world. It is the allusion to an annoying rain that initiates the segment that presents Susana installed in Pedro Páramo's house, also introducing the reader to Justina, who has been caring for Susana from her infancy. The narrative voice comments on a fine, persistent rain, which is quite different from the downpours of the Comala valley (155). Justina presumably has gone to buy herbs from the Indians, who have come from Opango to sell their goods. The reader sees her with an umbrella. "Venía por la calle derecha que viene de la Media Luna," explains a narrative voice, "rodeando los charcos que borbotaban sobre las banquetas" (156). On returning from her errand and entering Susana's room, the reader understands that Pedro Páramo has finally managed to seize Susana San Juan in an effort to capture a glimpse of his past. "Cuando venga Pedro Páramo," says Justina, "le diré que ya no te aguanto. Le diré que me voy" (158). That segment ends with a disturbing image of coldness and water rushing:

> Las sábanas estaban frías de humedad.
> Los caños borbotaban, hacían espuma,
> cansados de trabajar durante el día,
> durante la noche, durante el día.
> El agua seguía corriendo, diluviando
> en incesantes burbujas. (158)

However, although some of the fragments that deal with Susana San Juan are associated with an unwelcome rain, Susana's image is frequently closer to light imagery. Light, whether it is natural or artificial, seems to point always to the image of Susana. This aspect is remarkably noticeable toward the end of the novel and it emerges clearly when Pedro Páramo is contemplating Susana under the light of an oil lamp. As the flame of the lamp weakens, Pedro Páramo realizes that the constant nightmares that interrupt her sleep are gradually weakening Susana. Hence Pedro Páramo draws a parallel between the light of the lamp and Susana's life: "Qué sucedería si ella también se apagara cuando se apagara la llama de aquella débil luz con que él la veía?" (171). The light motif appears again after Susana has died and Pedro Páramo has decided to remain "sentado en un equipal" (188). He is then alone, outside and unable to sleep. The ominous character, who has become old and empty like Comala, is perhaps waiting for his death from Abundio Martínez's knife. His monologue flows:

> Hace mucho tiempo que te fuiste, Susana.
> La luz era igual entonces que ahora, no tan
> bermeja; pero era la misma pobre luz sin lumbre,
> envuelta en el paño blanco de la neblina que hay
> ahora. Era el mismo momento. Yo aquí, junto a la
> puerta mirando el amanecer y mirando cuando te ibas,
> siguiendo el camino del cielo; por donde el cielo
> comenzaba a abrirse en luces, alejándote, cada vez
> más desteñida entre las sombras de la tierra. (188)

The concept of light is reiterated in the paragraph as the reader sees Susana's image disappearing into space. Similar associations involving the light of the moon emerge only five paragraphs before Pedro Páramo disintegrates as if he were a pile of rocks. The monologue recites:

> ...Había una luna grande en medio del mundo.
> Se me perdían los ojos mirándote. Los rayos de la
> luna filtrándose sobre tu cara. No me cansaba de ver
> esa aparición que eras tú. Suave, restregada de luna;
> tu boca abullonada, humedecida, irisada de estrellas;
> tu cuerpo transparentándose en el agua de la noche.
> Susana, Susana San Juan. (194)

It is evident that Pedro Páramo could never really have his Dulcinea, Susana San Juan. After waiting thirty years for her, he finally obtains her by killing her father. But when he finds her, she is already detached from reality and lives obsessed with the erotic memories of Florencio, a man whom she calls her husband. Hence, Susana San Juan has become unapproachable to Pedro Páramo. (167, 170, 184). Poetic justice is achieved through this character, for she serves as the means of revenge for all the women whom Pedro Páramo violates and all the men who have suffered his outrage (Cobo Borda 38). In the last moments of his life Pedro Páramo feels her as distant from him as the celestial bodies that he is contemplating.

There are other characters and events in the narrative that are associated with heavenly bodies. A case in point is Miguel Páramo whose death is temporally and symbolically related to shooting stars falling from heaven. The first occurrence of this happening takes place after his funeral, when some farm hands are talking about the event and viewing it with bold cynicism. Terencio Lubianes, for example, says that Miguel's death hurt him a lot, for his shoulders still ache from carrying his weight (94); another man claims that his bunions have become enlarged because of Pedro Páramo's order that everyone wear shoes to the funeral. As this strange dialogue proceeds, a narrative voice interrupts with the following comment: "Había estrellas fugaces. Caían como si el cielo estuviera lloviznando lumbre" (94). As the sky seems to be producing multiple tiny sparks, the men resume their conversation in a joking mood and claim that up in the sky Miguel is having a welcoming reception with a fireworks display. Padre Rentería, who is at his home, also sees the shooting stars, but he interprets the phenomenon as a reproach from heaven, for he has favored the evildoers, namely Pedro Páramo, who has bought him with his wealth. Padre Rentería conducts a religious funeral for Miguel Páramo and pleads for his soul, although that criminal has violated Ana, his niece, after having assassinated her father. Padre Rentería is so uneasy with his conscience that he can't sleep and leaves his room in search of peace. A narrator comments then:

> Salió afuera y miró el cielo. Llovían estrellas.
> Lamentó aquello porque hubiera querido ver un
> cielo quieto. Oyó el canto de los gallos. Sintió la
> envoltura de la noche cubriendo la tierra, "este valle
> de lágrimas." (97)

The reader remains with the impression that Padre Rentería, like all the characters in the novel, will never rest in peace in that true vale of tears that is Comala. It is not surprising that the priest's remorse prompts him to join the revolt of the Cristeros (187).

Although Pedro Páramo is an intricate piece of fiction, which is charged with signs that point in different directions, it contains functional climatological and celestial referents that assist the reader in the elucidation of some of the puzzles it presents. The presence of heat is not only a sign of evil but aids in understanding Juan Preciado's strange death from the lack of breathable air. The allusions to water, in addition to announcing the register of characters like Pedro Páramo, are signs of the presence of the insane Susana San Juan. Other motifs like the light and the stars are useful microtextual references which aid in making associations in regard to events and characters. Moreover, these explicit atmospheric motifs, as they recur, constitute valuable elements of unity in the work.

Notes

1. The English translation of this quote is mine, as is the translation of the lines quoted from Sergio Fernández (1989).
2. See the explanation that Rulfo gives in regard to the selection of the name Comala in Reina Roffe's *Autobiografía armada* (Buenos Aires: Corregidor, 1973), 61. Cited by José Carlos González Boixo in his edition of *Pedro Páramo* (Madrid: Ediciones Cátedra, S.A., 1988), 64.

Works Cited

Cobo Borda, J.G. "Juan Rulfo y su murmullo inagotable." *Escritura* 10.19-20 (1985): 33-43.
Fernández, Sergio. *"Pedro Páramo:* una sesion espiritista." *Revista Iberoamericana* 55.148-149 (1989): 953-63.
Rulfo, Juan. *El llano en llamas*. México: Fondo de Cultura Económica, 1953.
———. *Pedro Páramo*. Ed. José Carlos González Boixo. Madrid: Ediciones Cátedra, S.A., 1988.
Volek, Emil. *"Pedro Páramo* de Juan Rulfo: una obra aleatoria en busca de su texto y del género literario." *Revista Iberoamericana* 56.150 (1990): 35-47.

 Ices Everlasting and Passions Perverted: The Physical and Moral Climates of Puig's Anti-utopia

Leonard A. Cheever

> But if it had to perish twice,
> I think I know enough of hate
> To say that for destruction ice
> Is also great
> And would suffice.
>
> Robert Frost, "Fire and Ice"

Manuel Puig's *Pubis Angelical* is a rich and complex work which examines the history, current status, and possible future direction of male/female relationships, with particular focus upon masculine domination and exploitation of women. Like the speaker in Yeats' "Sailing to Byzantium" wishes to do, the voices in Puig's novel speak forcefully and movingly "of what is past, or passing, or to come" in highly poetic language—especially in the novel's third part. Indeed, Part III of *Pubis Angelical* legitimately may be regarded as an extended metaphor in which Puig delineates a cold and inhospitable physical climate that mirrors and underscores the frigidly sterile and inhumanly perverted emotional climate of relationships between the sexes. Such a metaphor is both appropriate and effective. Clearly, Part III is designed to cause the reader to imagine a fantastic anti-utopian future which, despite its obvious unreality, nevertheless follows logically from a known past and a familiar present. Thus if Lakoff and Johnson are right in their assertion that metaphor is essential to *all* human thought (3-9), and consequently to our understanding of both past and present, then it seems only reasonable to assume that metaphors also are crucial in attempts to imagine any possible future. Therefore, I will examine both the nature and the implications of the extended metaphor Puig employs in Part III of his novel.

The novel's first and second parts set the stage for the metaphor employed in Part III. Part I, which begins in Europe in the 1930s, is a study of sexual enslavement, an enslavement so perverse, ubiquitous, and unyielding that one would have to turn to the fantasies of the Marquis de Sade or a work such as *The Story of O* to find any meaningful parallels. Not surprisingly, then, the moral atmosphere of Part I is not much different from that of a battlefield or an arena for gladiatorial combat. The central character, "the most beautiful woman in the world" (3), is held a virtual slave by her wealthy husband; she escapes from him through the aid of another man, who then betrays and exploits her, and she arrives finally in Hollywood where she becomes a famous actress. Ironically, however, her fame and "freedom" are meaningless because they are purchased at the price of still another kind of enslavement, this time at the hands of an unscrupulous producer. And thus she remains profoundly unhappy; she is constantly aware of her status as sex object, victim of exploitation, and literal or virtual slave to a seemingly endless succession of rapacious males. At one point she reads a phony "interview" put out by the movie studio's publicity department, and she reacts as follows:

> The text seemed almost a mockery, it told of her independent spirit, of the sheer enjoyment she had from working and providing for her own needs, and last of her happiness in California.... She then asked herself if... readers wouldn't have preferred to know the truth, that she had been manipulated all her life by forces of evil... that she had always been placed in deluxe glass showcases for the delight of the passers-by, that she had been dressed and undressed by cold hands which respected her as much as they would a mannequin. (92-93)

This woman's tragic story ends soon afterward in Mexico, where she is murdered by a rival actress.

Part I is thus a non-realistic narrative; it tells, primarily through visual images, a far-fetched and exaggerated story but, as several critics have observed, it is loosely based upon the experiences of a real person, actress Hedy Lamarr (Kerr 255n), and thus we may assume that the story's moral atmosphere, if not its specific details, is intended to be realistic and essentially accurate. For although Puig employs here the language, imagery, and stage effects of "Grade B" Hollywood films of the 1930s, it is clear that the theme of sexual exploitation is to be taken seriously, and consequently that Part I serves as a kind of archetypal account of the nature of male/female relationships during the first half of this century. Conversely, Part II is set in the mid-1970s; the mode of presentation is dramatic rather than narrative, dialogue and stream of consciousness (diary entries) replace the visual imagery of Part I, and the story told here is scrupulously realistic. However, the theme of Part II is precisely the same as that of Part I—and so is the moral atmosphere.

Ana, the central character of Part II, is a young Argentine expatriate who suffers from cancer and is confined to a Mexican hospital. Unlike the actress of Part I, she seems to be a relatively "liberated" woman. She has divorced a sexist and manipulative husband, is estranged from her mother and daughter (and thus from stereotypical "female" roles), and is determined not to fall into the same kinds of "traps" that previously have enveloped her. But she also is a profoundly unhappy woman. Like the cancer which threatens her life, her memories of her past relationships with men gnaw at her ceaselessly, and her only two friends in Mexico, a woman named Beatriz and an ex-lover named Pozzi, try to exploit her by enlisting her in their narrow, monomaniacal "causes": radical feminism in the former case, and leftist politics in the latter. Moreover, as Norman Lavers has observed, Ana still fantasizes that somewhere there is a "perfect" man who alone can make life worth living (46). In short, Ana is not "liberated" at all and, ironically, the only two alternatives to the traditional female roles presented to her (radical feminism or political fanaticism) are shown merely to be invitations to other kinds of exploitation. Therefore, since Puig has said on several occasions that he intended his book to be a "feminist" novel ("Interview" 226), it is not surprising that his work was misunderstood and/or rejected in terms of its original purpose; Puig has expressed his disappointment with the book's reception in the following terms:

> There was a strong feminist group in Mexico when I was living there. It was a difficult time. I showed them *Pubis Angelical* and they said, "We are not going to endorse your book because your character is not a role model." They wanted a strong woman to show them what to do. I think that was very stupid on their part. What the book tries to show is how difficult it is for a sincere woman to deal with the values of the past. Meanness and stupidity grow like weeds. (227)

Puig might have added that perhaps the Mexican feminists also were annoyed by the fact that Ana does not regard women as in any way ethically or morally superior to men; in a world at war, the book suggests, neither side, oppressor or oppressed, can lay any claim to moral superiority. In other words, an atmosphere of hostility and mutual incomprehension and contempt between men and women, an atmosphere that produces inevitably a moral climate in which *any* savagery against the "enemy" is permissible, hardly can be expected to engender virtue and harmony. And Ana is fully aware of that fact; in her final diary entry, after acknowledging that "I'm never going to understand [men], to me they are creatures from another planet" (195), she reflects:

> But the world is theirs. Even the Pope is a man, the politicians, the scientists. And the world is like that. The world is created in their image and likeness. Everything so dehumanized, so ugly, so rough .... A world of wars, of hysterical attacks between nations, of the exploitation of the weak ....
>
> I can't imagine a world governed by women. Because what we have in our heads are dresses, and curtains, and table cloths, and boots by Dior, and wallets by Gucci . . . and watches by Cartier .... What else do we women have in our heads? (197-98)

It is obvious from this passage that Ana has no illusions about any possible change for the better in terms of male/female relationships; even if women were to become dominant, she implies, there would be no reason to suppose that selfishness, exploitation, and mutual torment would instantly disappear. And clearly she cannot even *imagine* such a reversal. But of course there is nothing in her rumination which suggests that conditions cannot become even *worse* than they already are, and it is just such a grim possibility that provides the subject matter for Part III.

The novel's third part begins on page 127, when the story of the actress is complete and that of Ana is about half over (the narrative alternates among the three stories, with that of the actress confined to the first half of the novel, Part III to the second half, and the story of Ana appearing in installments throughout the entire text). By this point the reader understands that Ana is a kind of spiritual descendant of the actress, and the realistic story of Ana is likely to end as negatively as did the romanticized tale of her spiritual "sister." It is clear that nothing essential has changed between the time of the actress and that of Ana. Therefore, by the time the reader reaches Part III, he knows that the emotional climate of antagonism between the sexes and the concomitant moral atmosphere of indifferent cruelty and even open hostility among human beings are major themes in the novel; and this knowledge prepares the reader for understanding the implications of the extended metaphor which dominates and informs the future world that Puig has envisioned.

Part III is set in the near future after a great cataclysm ("The Great Turn of the Page") permanently has altered the earth's climate; as a consequence of this disaster [which occurred in "the year zero of the polar age," (128)], the earth is cold and bleak because "a change in the planet's rotational axis had been enough for vivid colors to disappear from nature and for the lands lately emerged to know only winter" (235). In fact, we are asked to imagine that the climatic calamity had been so complete that "all vegetation had died during the thaws, and the polar age had not seen the growth of a single blade of grass" (176). Nor surprisingly, then, human society and human relationships also have degenerated radically; governments are rigidly authoritarian, human freedom no longer exists, and the kind of enslavement pictured in the novel's first part has been institutionalized, has been made universal and systematic, and thus has been rendered infinitely more appalling and oppressive than it was shown to be in Part I. And of course women have become *sexual* as well as social and political slaves; only two roles for women are mentioned within the "new world order" of the polar age: all attractive young females are forced to spend a year as public concubines, i.e., as sex partners for old men; then they serve a second year ministering to the sexual needs of "crippled youths and deformed youths respectively, all of whom were beneficiaries under the statute for sexual services" (133). And concerning unattractive females, we are told only that "the ugly ones save themselves and get sent to work in the fields" (132). Thus harlotry and drudgery are presented as the two poles of existence for females during the "polar" age, and physical attractiveness (very clearly a subjective judgment made by males) is shown to be the sole criterion in determining which option is available to a given person. In short, it is difficult to imagine a more sexist, chauvinistic, or perversely arbitrary society than that of Puig's "polar age."

Obviously, then, Part III of *Pubis Angelical* serves as a kind of nightmare in which the conditions of the actress of Part I and Ana of Part II are stripped to their essentials and grotesquely exaggerated so as to reveal their true nature. And the physical climate which serves as the background for Part III thus becomes an extended metaphor which reflects and underscores those conditions. If we think of a metaphor in the traditional sense of "saying one thing and meaning another," then clearly the physical climate of Part III provides a way of speaking figuratively about the essential nature of male/female relationships in the past and present, and thus about the quality of the moral atmosphere surrounding those relationships. It is almost as if Puig is saying in Part III: "If you want fully to understand how awful relationships between the sexes were and are, imagine a world in which they have become institutionalized and thus clearly visible—but in order to do that you will have to imagine that nature itself has been perverted so that it corresponds metaphorically to the perversion at the heart of such relationships." In other words, the reader must imagine the world as being physically different from what it is if he or she is fully to perceive how it actually has been (Part I) and continues to be (Part II) in terms of male/female antagonism and mutual predation. Thus in Puig's metaphor the imaginary world of the future becomes the figurative touchstone which reveals a crucial fact about the real world of the past and present; Samuel R. Levin has adumbrated how such metaphors may function in a literary text in the following terms:

> [G]iven an incompatibility between [an] utterance and conditions in the world, [in ordinary metaphor] the conditions are to be taken as fixed, and it is the utterance that must be construed. Now this is not a logically necessary position. We may, if we like, assume that, in the face of an incompatibility between what is asserted in an utterance

and conditions as they obtain in the world, we regard the utterance as fixed and construe the world. Instead, that is, of construing the utterance so that it makes sense in the world, [in literary metaphors] we construe the world so as to make sense of the utterance. (131)

In the sense of Puig's text, the "utterance" in question is nothing more or less than the theme of Parts I and II, i.e., the proposition that human beings live in an environment of antagonism and mutual hostility due to human sexuality, and thus that sexuality itself is the ultimate cause of frustration, unhappiness, and tragic and wasted lives. But the narrative of Part I and the drama of Part II are set in the real world that we all are familiar with; the problem is not to "construe" that world itself, but rather to find *human* (subjective) meaning and significance within it. And any such meaning or significance remains figurative (metaphorical) in the sense that it reflects how we judge, evaluate, or interpret the real world; in other words, it gives insight into what we as humans make of the world rather than into what the world really is from any conceivable objective, non-human perspective. Max Black identifies the production of such insight as one of the most powerful functions of metaphor when he asserts, "Metaphors . . . can, and sometimes do, generate insight about 'how things are' in reality" (41). Black has in mind ordinary metaphors in which reality is taken as fixed, and thus the utterance (subjective, non-literal judgment or interpretation) requires construal, but clearly literary metaphors, such as the one Puig employs in Part III of *Pubis Angelical*, also can generate insight into 'how things are' in reality once we realize that it is the world that must be construed rather than the utterance which embodies its human meaning and significance.

We may conclude, therefore, that Part III constitutes a lyric meditation upon what the world *becomes* if we accept the proposition that human sexuality is such an essential (and negative) factor in our experience of reality that it literally has the power to convert reality into the non-literal term in a metaphor, a metaphor in which sexuality serves as the fixed or literal term. Such a conclusion may seem, on the face of it, wrong-headed and perverse; however, it is fully in keeping with certain concepts which modern science takes seriously in its ongoing attempts to understand and to explain reality. For example, O. B. Hardison, Jr., observes that

> science [once] believed that it could present man with truth. This was a fantasy. Science still challenges religion and mythology and tradition . . . but it no longer promises to replace them with truth, only with necessary fictions . . . . [Because there] is a widespread sense that the world as it is known is a construct. If there is an absolute reality—a *real* reality—it is known only as a tantalizing, ever-receding goal. (48-49)

Elsewhere Hardison examines the idea of "reality as game" (47) and speaks of the concept "that nature is infinitely complicated and variable. It can never be 'observed.' It can only be approximated . . . [because] reality is partly our own creation, and what we see in it is partly the shape of our own motives" (60-61). In the light of Hardison's observations, the idea of the real world as the non-literal element in a metaphor (i.e., as that which must be construed) does not appear as odd as it otherwise might seem; moreover, the concepts Hardison mentions are not essentially different from the one implicit in Henry James' famous dictum, written in 1884, which asserts that "you will not write a good novel unless you possess the sense of reality; but . . . reality has myriad forms" (393). Very clearly, Part III of *Pubis Angelical* may be viewed as an exploration of one of the "myriad forms" of reality generated by the implacable fact of human sexuality.

Finally, then, we also may conclude that the bleak and frigid physical climate of the novel's third part is an appropriate metaphor for the moral atmosphere of the "polar age" of human sexuality. As Pamela Bacarisse has observed, the story of W218, the "public concubine" who serves as the heroine of Part III, is merely an extension and intensification of those of the actress and Ana—and the fact that W218 lives in a Mexico City of the future reiterates the connection between the three characters (140-43). However, W218's fate is even worse than that of her spiritual "ancestors." After attempting to murder the man who has betrayed her, she is condemned for life to the far-off penal colony of "Ices Everlasting" where she will be required to perform her sexual "services" with disease-ridden inmates, and thus will face certain death as well as total degradation (218-19). Marta Morello-Frosch has argued that the very concept of a place such as "Ices Everlasting" ties together the themes of political repression and sexual hostility and exploitation in a markedly effective way:

> En un mundo deshumanizado, homogeneizado y gratificante en sus más mínimos aspectos, incluso y principalmente en el campo sexual, se ha logrado reducir los antagonismos sociales de los protagonistas a cambio de una aceptación total de directivas superiores . . . [y al mismo tiempo] el romance de W218 parece indicar que la política de su país ha sido determinada por fenómenos naturales tales como la emergencia de la era glacial y la resultante desaparición de formas vegetales y sociales. La narración evoca formas reconocibles de opresión en países totalitarios modernos, incluso la presencia de la vigilancia constante, el destierro a Siberias ficticias, y hasta un pabellón de cáncer donde sirven los condenados por desacato. Pero el impulso que genera las acciones sigue siendo el erotismo mal dirigido del personaje . . . . (37-38)

Professor Morello-Frosch's obvious allusions to works such as Solzhenitsyn's *Gulag Archipelago* and *Cancer Ward* are perhaps instructive as to why readers may find Part III of *Pubis Angelical* disturbingly moving and effective, for even readers who have never been exiled to Siberia or suffered from cancer can be powerfully moved by Solzhenitsyn's works. And since that is the case, clearly *literal* exile to a place such as "Ices Everlasting" is not a prerequisite for understanding the kind of moral atmosphere the perversion of human sexuality may produce—or for imagining that such an atmosphere ultimately might alter the very climate of our world.

Works Cited

Bacarisse, Pamela. *The Necessary Dream: A Study of the Novels of Manuel Puig.* Tontowa, NJ: Barnes & Noble, 1988.

Black, Max. "More about Metaphor." *Metaphor and Thought.* Ed. Andrew Ortony. Cambridge, Eng.: Cambridge University Press, 1979. 19-43.

Hardison, O. B., Jr. *Disappearing through the Skylight: Culture and Technology in the Twentieth Century.* New York: Viking, 1989.

James, Henry. "The Art of Fiction." *Criticism: The Major Statements.* Ed. Charles Kaplan. New York: St. Martin's, 1986. 386-404.

Kerr, Lucille. *Suspended Fictions: Reading the Novels of Manuel Puig.* Urbana: Univeresity of Illinois Press, 1987.

Lakoff, George, and Johnson, Mark. *Metaphors We Live By.* Chicago: University of Chicago Presss, 1980.

Lavers, Norman. *Pop Culture Into Art: The Novels of Manuel Puig.* Columbia, University of Missouri Press, 1988.

Levin, Samuel R. "Standard Approaches to Metaphor and a Proposal for Literary Metaphor." *Metaphor and Thought.* Ed. Andrew Ortony. Cambridge, Eng.: Cambridge University Press, 1979, 136-47.

Morello-Frosch, Marta. "Usos y abusos de la cultura popular: *Pubis angelical* de Manuel Puig." *Literature and Popular Culture in the Hispanic World.* Ed. Rose S. Minc. Upper Montclair, NJ: Montclair State College, Ediciones Hispamérica, 1981. 31-42.

Puig, Manuel. "Interview." *Interviews with Latin American Writers.* Ed. Marie-Lise Gazarian Gautier. Elmwood Park, IL: Dalkey Archive Press, 1989, 219-33.

———. *Pubis Angelical.* Trans. Elena Brunet. New York: Aventura, 1986.

 Influence of Climate on the Cultures of the Jungle as Perceived by Two Latin American Novelists

Raquel Romeu

> Differences in [climate] patterns from place to place, and changes in them from time to time, have inevitably exerted a powerful influence on human affairs. They define regions in which man must exert special efforts to avoid freezing or roasting to death.... Climate, along with soil (which is itself heavily influenced by climate), determines what plants can flourish and thus what animals—including man—can survive by eating the plants, or one another (Claiborne 26).

Robert Claiborne in *Climate, Man, and History* also differentiates among four basic types of climates: polar, cold and dry; stormy, warm or cold depending on the season, but quite humid at all times; desert, very hot and dry; and equatorial, very hot and wet. In this last group is the Amazon basin where we find the two primitive cultures presented by Alejo Carpentier and Mario Vargas Llosa in their respective novels: *The Lost Steps* (*Los pasos perdidos*, 1962) and *The Storyteller* (*El hablador*, 1987).

In the first novel, Carpentier describes a village of the Guahibo Indians located on a channel (caño) of the Orinoco system, and the Shirishana tribe who live along the upper Caura, a tributary of the same river. In the second novel, Vargas Llosa introduces the reader to the Machiguenga, a tribe scattered throughout the region of the Madre de Dios and upper Urubamba rivers in the Amazon system. Both novels are the result of trips into the jungle which left a strong impression upon these writers. A new world totally unknown to them had unfolded before their eyes.[1]

Surprise, amazement, incredulity mark Carpentier's first encounter, in the remote jungle, with man living still in that second level that Claiborne calls barbarism. This is the stage where man already plants certain staples and raises some domestic animals, but still supplements his diet of meat by hunting. These groups live in this very hot and humid equatorial climate, in semi-permanent villages inhabited by just a few hundred souls.

Concerning groups classified as savages or barbarians, Claiborne observes that the Bushmen of Australia are less savage than almost any civilized nation and that they call themselves "the harmless people" (234). In *The Lost Steps* the narrator recalls the extermination of the Jews in the Nazi concentration camps during World War II and makes the same observation as Claiborne.

The primitive man of the Amazon basin, or rather, this man perfectly adapted to his surroundings, has survived in his isolation and the environment in which he lives has survived with him. Meggers says in *Amazonia*: "aboriginal man appears to have been no more destructive than his fellow organisms to the long-term stability of the tropical rain forest ecosystem" (150).

The jungle could not logically have been the cradle of civilization. Carpentier's narrator reinforces this theory when, penetrating into the heart of the jungle through a narrow channel (caño), he describes a setting that reminds the reader of the original chaos from which the world as we know it today sprang: "One felt the presence of rampant fauna, of the primeval slime, of the green fermentation beneath the dark waters, which gave off a sour reek like a mud of vinegar and carrion . . ." (160).[2]

Minute descriptions depict the "real" jungle as an asphyxiating place in constant state of decay: the asphyxiating climate of the equatorial regions. In the midst of such an environment, viewed as hostile by the narrator, the Guahibo Indians appear perfectly adapted to this milieu: "in their own surroundings . . . they were complete masters of their culture . . . The fact that they ignored many things that to me were basic and necessary was a far cry from putting them in the category of primitive beings" (173).[3]

Carpentier's narrator marvels at the precision with which one has caught a fish by putting an arrow through it; how another uses a blowgun; or the technique of a group covering the framework of a longhouse with palm fronds. They reveal themselves as "masters of the skills required on the stage of their existence" (173).[4] But it is the climate that is ultimately responsible for the setting of the "stage."

As the narrator pushes farther into the different climates of the South American continent, he also recedes in time. If the Guahibo culture had amazed him, his encounter with the Shirishana Indians of the upper Caura leads him to believe that he has arrived at the first stage of human life:

> We had emerged from the Paleolithic . . . to enter a state that pushed the limits of human life back to the darkest murk of the night of ages. These beings I saw now with legs and arms that resembled mine . . . these people still without the primordial shame

that leads to the concealment of the organs of generation, who were naked without knowing it . . . were nevertheless men (181-82).[5]

These people, who have not yet discovered seeds, do not stay in one place, but wander aimlessly, eating whatever they can find. They fight the monkeys for palm hearts, climbing high up in the trees ("colgándose de las techumbres de la selva," 243). When isolated by floods for long periods, they have eaten "the larvae of wasps, munched ants, lice, dug into the earth for worms and maggots" (182) and eaten even the earth itself. Fire is almost unknown to them and their dogs resemble primitive pre-dogs ("perros anteriores a los perros").

The narrator doubts that he can communicate with them, even by gestures. The infra-human appears when the Adelantado, a character who has made his home in the jungle where he has founded a city—like the early Conquistadores—points out to the narrator the prisoners of the Shirishanas in a muddy hole that looks like a dirty pigpen full of gnawed bones. "I saw before me the most horrible things my eyes had ever beheld" (182). He calls them "fetuses with white beards" and "wrinkled dwarfs" (182).

These "human larvae" were captives of the Shirishanas, who believed themselves to be the superior race, the only rightful owners of the jungle. Horrified at this vision, the narrator asks himself if there might be yet other lower groups that, in turn, might have prisoners of their own whom they might consider their inferiors.

The Machiguengas presented by Vargas Llosa in *The Storyteller* also consider themselves the sole owners of the jungle. They call themselves "the men." It seems to be a human trait for each ethnic group, regardless of cultural level, to consider itself the chosen people.

While Carpentier's prose is exuberant like the jungle he describes, Vargas Llosa sketches with tight strokes and unique language structure a way of life. Alien to our Western culture, this life is, nonetheless, very real in the jungles of Peru where the oppressive climate allows no alternative:

> . . . three or four photographs . . . suddenly brought back to me the flavor of the Peruvian jungle. The wide rivers, the enormous trees, the fragile canoes, the frail huts raised up on pilings, and the knots of men and women, naked to the waist and daubed with paint, looking at me unblinkingly from the glossy prints.[6] (3)

For Carpentier life in the equatorial climate contrasts with life in the great city, New York, where Western culture prevails and from which the narrator turns in disgust. Traveling to the jungle in search of certain musical instruments, supposedly the first which man had invented, the narrator really seeks his own identity. He is a man trapped between two cultures: the European, representative of our Western world; and the Latin American, that, depending on the climate, will have retained the romantic flavor of the nineteenth century, or will have remained in the Middle Ages or some earlier time. Once in the jungle, he imagines he has found what he had lost in the civilized world. The simple life, love without complications and the absolute disregard of time bring incentive and inspiration back into his life and make it meaningful again.

The novelist's approach combines personal and cultural elements. Much of the story in *The Lost Steps* has an autobiographical basis. America, especially Cuba and the Caribbean region, became an obsession with Carpentier, occupying the settings of his novels and short stories. Yet culturally he was very French, very European in his point of view. He underlines this fact with a profusion of quotes and literary, philosophical, and historical intertextual references to Western culture.

Vargas Llosa, whose novel *The Storyteller* appeared twenty five years after *The Lost Steps,* was educated in the Latin American pattern, never traveling to Europe until after completing his studies at Lima's University of San Marcos. His preoccupation with America centers upon Peru and Peruvian social problems. Vargas Llosa's interest in his country's well-being led to his becoming a presidential candidate in the 1990 Peruvian elections, although he had never participated in politics before and was, instead, completely dedicated to literature. The very fact that he decided to enter the political arena speaks of his great concern for his country, a sentiment profoundly coloring *The Storyteller.*

The diversity of climates in Peru and other South American countries generally has resulted in a plurality of cultures, producing serious economic, political and even moral problems, besides the cultural ones.

In *The Storyteller,* Saúl Zuratas and Mario Vargas Llosa (speaking as another character), represent divergent opinions with respect to the problem of jungle cultures in Peru.

> ... those compatriots of ours who from time immemorial had lived there, harassed and grievously harmed, between the wide, slow rivers, dressed in loincloths and marked with tattoos, worshipping the spirits of trees, snakes, clouds, and lightning.... (13)[7]

In *A Writer's Reality* (1991), Vargas Llosa has declared that if he were forced to choose between preserving the Indian jungle cultures or decreeing their complete assimilation, he would, with great sorrow opt for the modernization of those tribes as the greatest urgency is to combat "hunger and misery." Concerning the Machiguenga tribe, he affirms that "their culture is alive in spite of the fact that it has been repressed and persecuted since Inca times" (36). They should perhaps be respected, but their fragile culture will not survive much longer. ". . . it is tragic to destroy what is still living, still a driving cultural possibility, even if it is archaic; but I am afraid we shall have to make a choice" (37).

Thus while Zuratas, alias Mascarita, defends the Machiguengas and their right to be respected in their jungle, the author speaks for those who believe in the need to sacrifice them in the name of progress.

Mascarita sees in the destruction of such cultures the destruction of the ecology. The white men (viracochas) and the Indians from the Andes mountains have come into the jungle at different times to clear the woods with fires burning large extensions of land; after planting one or two crops the soil has been rendered barren for lack of humus and because of the erosion caused by the rain. Animals have been exterminated because of the greed for hides; some species are disappearing rapidly. Not only is this happening in Peru, but in Brazil large portions of the rain forest have been pointlessly destroyed. The earth is now incapable of producing anything. In the equatorial climates the jungle thrives, but stripped of it the soil becomes barren.

Vargas Llosa first became aware of life in the jungle and its problems in 1957 during his first trip there, discovering a face of his country of which he had been totally ignorant. He, like Carpentier when speaking of Venezuela, comes to the conclusion that Peru is a country of many climates and many cultures: a country of the twentieth century, but also of the Middle Ages and of the Stone Age. His first impression of the Peruvian jungle recalls the reaction of Carpentier: "narrow river channels so choked with tangled vegetation overhead that in bright daylight it seemed dark as night" (72).

These Machiguengas that live around the Madre de Dios and upper Urubamba rivers are isolated, living in little groups of families and moving progressively deeper into the jungle, driven away by the viracochas and more warlike tribes. At different times there have been booms known as fevers, "fiebres." Rubber, gold, rosewood and agricultural colonization have attracted those who have pushed them into more unhealthy and infertile regions where they live in tiny family nuclei without villages or chiefs.

By one of those remote rivers on the Amazon system, the Timpinía, the storyteller finds a Machiguenga family who have built their little camp in that isolated spot. When he arrives to spend a few days with the family, he is greeted with great joy, and they converse at length. The Machiguengas are noted for being great conversationalists. Tasurinchi-el de Timpinía, the head of the family, complains to Tasurinchi-hablador, the storyteller, that in those lands one can only plant a couple of times in the same place, no more. Sometimes only once. "It's land that tires quickly, it appears. It wants me to leave it in peace . . . . This earth here along the Timpinía is lazy" (221).[8]

A tremor occurs while the wife is alone in the camp. When the husband returns and she tells him, he beats her up because he thinks she is lying. And then, there is another tremor. Tasurinchi from Timpinía decides this needs much meditation. He goes off and sits on a rock all night and all morning. Toward midday he has found an explanation for that geophysical sign. He must move his family to another location. He tells the storyteller:

> I remembered something I knew when I was born... Or perhaps I learned it in a trance. If an evil occurs on the earth, it's because people have stopped paying attention to the earth, because they don't look after it the way it ought to be looked after. Can it talk the way we do? To say what it wants to say, it has to do something. Shake, perhaps. To say: Don't forget me. To say: I'm alive, too. I don't want to be ill-treated. (226)[9]

Saúl Zuratas considers the cultures of Amazonia well equipped to deal with their surroundings, possessing a subtle and profound knowledge of things we, the civilized people, have forgotten: the relation between man and nature and, also, between man and God. That harmony we have "shattered forever."

While employing different perspectives, both writers coincide with Claiborne who believes that

> The dinosaurs and every creature that ever lived, or now lives, on earth, had adapted to their environment—flourishing when the adaptation was adequate to the circumstances, disappearing when it was not. Only man, with the aid of his brain, can adapt the environment to himself. He is the only creature, for instance, that can manipulate climate, even on a small scale. He is also the only creature that can wonder about it or write books about it. (78)

But Carpentier's narrator, after having retraced man's steps back to the Fourth Day of Creation, loses that paradise forever, by returning to our Western world. He will not find the way back. For him, the artist, the composer, it was impossible to rid himself of his cultural baggage.

By contrast, Vargas Llosa's character, Saúl Zuratas, alias Mascarita, voluntarily renounces his Western culture, erasing all traces of his previous life and emerging fully in the Machiguenga world as Tasurinchi—the storyteller. His absolute transformation, like a rebirth, renders him a true Machiguenga possessing the power of the word that transmits the group's beliefs, legends, and their history.

In both novels our world, that of the stormy climate where our Western civilization thrives, is conceived as a totally different world, apart from that of the equatorial climate. In order to integrate them one must be sacrificed: the more fragile, but in doing so, the climate might be altered, which may endanger gravely the ecological stability of our planet.

Notes

1. Carpentier visited the jungle twice during his long stay in Caracas. In July, 1947, he traveled in the direction of Guyana. In September, 1948, he made a second trip, this time up the Orinoco arriving at a village that he calls Santa Mónica de los Venados in the novel. It was on this last trip that he encountered the Guahibo and Shirishana tribes.

2. "Se adivinaba la cercanía de toda una fauna rampante, del lodo eterno, de la glauca fermentación, debajo de aquellas aguas oscuras que olían agriamente, como un fango que hubiera sido amasado con vinagre y carroña..." (223). All quotes appear in translation in the text and in the original in an endnote. Both are from the editions cited.

3. "Aquellos indios... me resultaban, en su ámbito, en su medio absolutamente dueños de su cultura.... La evidencia de que desconocían cosas que eran para mí esenciales y necesarias, estaba muy lejos de vestirlos de primitivismo" (234).

4. "... maestro[s] en la totalidad de oficios propiciados por el teatro de su existencia"(234).

5. Hemos salido del paleolítico... para entrar en un ámbito que [hace] retroceder los confines de la vida humana a lo más tenebroso de la noche de las edades. Esos individuos con piernas y brazos que veo ahora, tan semejantes a mí... esas gentes que aún no han cobrado el pudor primordial de ocultar los órganos de la generación, que están desnudos sin saberlo... son hombres, sin embargo (243).

6. ... tres o cuatro fotografías... me devolvieron, de golpe, el sabor de la selva peruana. Los anchos ríos, los corpulentos árboles, las frágiles canoas, las endebles cabañas sobre pilotes, y los almácigos [?] de hombres y mujeres, semidesnudos y pintarrajeados, contemplándome fijamente desde sus cartulinas brillantes (7).

7. ... esos compatriotas nuestros que desde tiempos inmemoriales vivían allá, acosados y lastimados, entre los anchos y lentos ríos, con taparrabos y tatuajes, adorando los espíritus del árbol, la serpiente, la nube y el relámpago... (15).

8. Es una tierra que se cansa pronto, parece. Está queriendo que la deje en paz... Tierras perezozas son éstas de Timpinía (223).

9. Me acordé de algo que nací sabiendo.... Si un daño ocurre en la tierra es porque la gente ya no le presta atención, porque no la cuida como hay que cuidarla. ¿Puede la tierra hablar, como nosotros? Para decir lo que quiere, algo tendrá que hacer. Temblar, quizás. No se olviden de mí, diciendo. Yo también vivo,... No quiero que me maltraten (217).

Works Cited

Carpentier, Alejo. *Los pasos perdidos*. Ed. Roberto González Echevarría. Madrid: Ediciones Cátedra, 1985.

———. *The Lost Steps*. Trans. by Harriet Onís. New York: Alfred A. Knopf, 1956.

Claiborne, Robert. *Climate, Man, and History*. New York: W. W. Norton, 1970.

Meggers, Betty Jane. *Amazonia: Man and Culture in a Counterfeit Paradise*. Chicago: Aldine-Atherton, 1971.

Vargas Llosa, Mario. *El hablador*. Barcelona: Editorial Seix Barral, 1987.

———. *The Storyteller*, translated by Helen Lane. New York: Farrar Straus Giroux, 1989.

———. *A Writer's Reality*. Ed. Myron I. Lichtblau. Syracuse: Syracuse University Press, 1991.

# Climate and Identity in the Literature of the French Antilles

Jack Jordan

While man's search for identity does not belong solely to the writers of Guadeloupe and Martinique, it does take on a character unique to these Caribbean islands. Because of the diversity of cultures which have come together to form these francophone societies and the composition of the prevailing winds, sun, water and volcanic landscape which make up the climate of these islands, a distinctive dialectic between culture and climate has been established which cannot be ignored in this search. As we shall see, the composing elements of this tropical climate evolve from playing a purely descriptive, exotic role in literature to become a character in themselves, offering a fundamental, unconscious unity in which the Antillean identity is submerged.

When we trace the ever-present yet changing role of climate in the literature of the French Antilles from its beginning to its present-day form, it is useful to divide the history of francophone literature of the Caribbean into three general periods. While these divisions can be criticized as an oversimplification which does not picture the overall complexity of this literature (e.g., by not specifically including the literature of the societies of the plantation owners, or "békés," the slaves, the mulattos, or the themes of rural versus city life, the surrealist and feminist influences, etc.), they do serve to illustrate in an orderly fashion the topic in question.

The first is the romantic or exotic period, extending from the middle of the nineteenth century through the twentieth century. This literature reflects the relative lack of importance the liberation of the black slaves in 1848 had on the culture of the islands. In 1850, Poirié de Saint-Aurèle describes his love for the Antilles: "I love our blue sea . . . warm suns . . . abundant light [and our] carefree, laughing negroes."[1]

Compared to the inviting tropical climate, the plight of the black slave had no importance. Daniel Thaly describes the exotic island of his birth:

> I was born on an island in love with the wind
> Where the air has the smells of sugar and vanilla
> and which cradles in the moving tropical sun
> the warm and blue currents of the Caribbean sea.[2]

The tropical climate is always friendly and inviting. There is little or no evidence of volcanic eruptions or hurricanes. Even in the poetry of Jean-Louis Baghio'o, the intrusion of the destructive forces which are inherent to the tropical climate is only a passing interruption to the tropical serenity of the islands. In his poem "Bourrasque," or "Squall," the sun disappears, the rain falls, the waters rise until finally, one of the ultimate destructive climatic forces of the Antilles appears. However, even in the despair resulting from the chaos following such a climatic experience, the tropical beauty returns to overpower the destruction wrought by the ephemeral squall. At last, the "parfums bruns" are once again spread by the seaspray, and paradise returns.

Full of warm seas and fresh marine breezes, this literature would be suitable for a tourist brochure and could have been conceived by a writer of the Caribbean, Europe, or North America, be he/she black or white. The search for identity has no place in the literary paradise of this period where man and nature are fused in the same purity and beauty. In his 1935 collection of poems in prose, "Parfums et saveurs des Antilles," André Thomarel reflects this fusion in his memories of "evenings padded with fresh and adorable marine breezes and silent walks on the thick carpet of sand . . . and the silk of her hair.[3]

While references to the exotic climate never disappear from the literature of the French Antilles, they take on a different form in the second period. However, before turning to the role of climate in the *negritude* movement, I must discuss briefly its origins and its meaning. The neologism "négritude" was coined in Paris with the publication of *L'étudiant noir* in 1934. The principal contributors were of diverse geographic origins: Léopold Senghor of Senegal, Léon-Gontran Damas of Guiana and Aimé Césaire of Martinique. Even in the diversity of its geographic origins one can see an effort towards a universally binding force which might give a foundation, or roots, to not only the black experience but, even more, to a common black cultural identity. It should be of no surprise that the source of this identity was found in Africa. As A. James Arnold states in *Modernism & Negritude: The Poetics of Aimé Césaire,* the "experience of being rooted in black history through African language and tribal customs was surely communicated to [Césaire] as an ideal relation to life, one of which West Indians had been deprived by reason of the combined effects of colonialism and slavery" (9).

It is ironic, however, that Césaire's principal source of information on black Africa was the writings of Leo Frobinius, a white European. Frobinius believed that the difference in the races has a biological foundation. The difference between a black and a white is to be found in their blood. He further postulated that black cultural traits can be transmitted through a racial, or ethnic memory. When Césaire stated in an October 1961 issue of the magazine *Afrique,* "I am an African poet" (Arnold 44), it would seem that, in spite of his West Indian background, he believes in this doctrine. The search for identity would seem to result here with an ethnic rooting in black Africa, without any concern for the diversity of culture found in North America, the Antilles, or Africa itself. As Arnold points out, however, "the postulate of an archaic ethnic memory is patently absurd, since it can operate only in conjunction with an ideal ethnic purity" (62). In truth, Césaire later disassociated himself with this notion of *negritude* based on an ethnic uniqueness, stating that Senghor, one of its principal proponents, "tended . . . to construct negritude into an essentialism as though there were a black essence, a black soul . . . but I never accepted this point of view" (Arnold 44). Instead, Césaire's works demonstrate a *negritude* simply based on the right to be black and affirm one's blackness. In fact, in studying the role of the climate and geography particular to the Antilles in Césaire's works, one sees that it is here that the Antillian identity is to be found and not in any racial memory rooted in Africa.

While the references to the tropical nature of the Antilles have sometimes been dismissed as simply a continuation of the exotic tendencies already discussed, the issue in Césaire's work is one not of exoticism, but of authenticity. Since Césaire is writing in French and not in the local creole, "it is only in this way that Césaire can remind the reader that he is not an ersatz Frenchman" (Arnold 91). Césaire's descriptions would probably not entice a would-be tourist to pick Martinique as a destination. In his *Notebook of A Return To The Native Land (Cahier d'un retour au pays natal)*, one finds a world "surveyed night and day by a cursed venereal sun" (35).[4] Hardly a paradise described in Club Med brochures, Martinique is, rather, "an aged poverty rotting under the sun, silently; an aged silence bursting with tepid pustules, the awful futility of our raison d'être" (35).[5] The lure of a peaceful, warm, romantic escape is nothing but "your aborted dreams, the river of life desperately torpid in its bed, neither turgid nor low, hesitant to flow, pitifully empty, the impartial heaviness of boredom distributing shade equally on all things, the air stagnant, unbroken by the brightness of a single bird" (41).[6] While there has been a tendency to insist on the universal or quasi-African nature of Césaire's writings, these quotes suggest instead an attempt to reveal the reality of Martinique. The "Native Land" he refers to is not Africa, but

Martinique. As J. Michael Dash points out: "Beneath the... balmy natural setting which is the traditional stereotype of the Caribbean, Césaire presents a dense field of relationships that allows the individual consciousness to grow with the discovery of landscape, akin to Claudel's notion of *co-naissance* (in which observer and observed coexist)" (*Discourse* xxxvi).

One of the most unusual aspects of both Guadeloupe and Martinique is their volcanoes—respectively La Soufrière and Mont Pelée. Landscape, climate and identity are fused in a way unique to these islands. One has only to hike up these sister volcanoes to understand the role they play in the climate of the islands. While dormant, the change in temperature from the beaches to the top of the crater can be as great as 10-20 degrees fahrenheit. Active, they provide one of the most dramatic—and deadly—climatic changes the islands experience. Their role in the francophone literature of the Antilles cannot be over-emphasized. When, in a 1977 interview, Césaire defines himself not as an African poet, but as one who is Martinique, he is speaking of the ever-present Mont Pelée: "I believe that I would define myself as being a man of the earth, of mountain and of fire. In my sensibility the mountain plays a very great role because I am a Martinican, and because at the horizon of the Martinican sensibility there is always the presence of the mountain."[7] Landscape, climate, identity—all explode, all undergo a "co-naissance" when Césaire describes what is no longer an exotic tropical paradise: ". . . the volcanoes will explode, the naked water will bear away the ripe sun stains and nothing will be left but a tepid bubbling pecked at by sea birds—the beach of dreams and the insane awakenings" (*Notebook* 35).[8] As we shall see in the discussion of the third period, this explosive unity of landscape, climate and identity will dominate the French literature of the Antilles.

During an interview I had with Maryse Condé in Guadeloupe last summer, I asked her her opinion concerning the negritude movement. Her response reflects that of other writers of the third, or creole period of the French literature of the Antilles:

> Recently there was a discussion with Césaire. He said that, "as long as there are blacks who think, negritude will exist." Me, I don't believe it. I believe, in fact, that to the extent that blacks reflect, they perceive . . . that Blacks don't exist. It's the racism of the whites that has made identical people out of all men with black skins, and you can imagine how all men with black skin had the same culture, the same expectations, perhaps even the same language, etc. One perceives, however, that the black world is completely diverse. There are *several* black peoples with different, particular histories, with different ambitions, different problems. And I believe that eventually one realizes that there can be no negritude, that is to say, a completely fluid community which bases itself on the color of individuals. I think that negritude is condemned. . . . And that what will appear will be regional literatures . . . which will take over the lead.[9]

While the "thrust of negritude among Caribbean intellectuals was [an effort] . . . to rediscover unity beyond dispersion" (*Discourse* 5), the writers of the third movement declare that "créolité" is "an annihilation of false universality, of monolinguism and of purity."[10] As a character in Daniel Maximin's *Lone Sun* (*L'Isolé Soleil*) states, "identification is the enemy of identity."[11] The native, non-intellectual Antillean never did get involved in this effort to identify with this vague notion of "Mother Africa." Asked by a local zombi what he was going to do with all the different races in his blood, Pipi, a character in Patrick Chamoiseau's *Chronical of Seven Miseries* (*Chronique des sept misères*) who had never asked himself the question, gives the classic negritude response. He would return to his roots in Africa. The zombi replies, "What? What Africa? . . . There's no more Africa. First of all, where is Africa? Where are the paths, the traces of a return? Are there memories of the road on the waves?"[12] Rather than forcing an identification with a far-away, theoretical, universalizing force of Africa, the creole movement emphasizes its diverse backgrounds and grounds itself in a "dialectic reestablished between nature and culture in the Caribbean" (*Discourse* 65).[13]

Like Pipi, the Caribbean writer of the Creole movement will remain in the Antilles to cultivate its own rich, tropical and diverse garden. Daniel Maximin also suggests both this breaking up of Leo Frobinius' theory and the taking root of the search for identity in the tropical nature of the Antilles when he has one of his characters establish what he refers to as his "frobénisme tropico-volcanique." In this theory, the Guadeloupeans "are of the Ethiopean sort, tranquil like the Soufrière, and the Martinicans are Hamitic, boiling like Pelée."[14] This theory, of course, is rejected as "jealous oversimplifications."[15] The creole search for identity, while emphasizing diversity, is not one of division, of individuality. It is a search not for an I, but a We: "We, the people of the Antilles, we are the debris of a synthesis."[16] It is the same for Eduard Glissant (*Discourse* xix) for whom the search is different from that of the classic European intellectual: "To the same extent that the Cartesian ego is decentered . . . Glissant elevates landscape to a central position in his discourse" (xxxvii).

The change from the negritude to the creole movement in the literature of the French Antilles is one from looking for identity in an abstract, unifying universal to rooting it in a cross-cultural poetics, itself inseparable from the climate and landscape unique to the islands. The search for identity is not static and one-directional, reaching for its roots in Africa. Rather, it is more like "submarine roots: that is, floating free, not fixed in one position in some primordial spot, but extending in all directions in our world through its network of branches" (*Discourse* 67).[17]

This free-floating search for identity that is at the heart of the literature of the French Antilles is a dynamic one, without clear-cut boundaries. It is a search without beginning or end, inseparable from the exotic yet explosive climate of these Caribbean islands: "No dénouement, above all no end: still thirst, with the fire of the heart and of the volcano, the wind of the cyclones and the kisses, the spring water and the sea."[18]

Notes

1. "J'aime notre mer bleue et sa tempête ardente: / J'aime des soleils chauds la lumière abondante / . . . Nos nègres sans soucis, nos négresses rieuses" (17). This and the following translations are mine.
2. "Je suis né dans une île amoureuse du vent
    Où l'air a des odeurs de sucre et de vanille
    Et que berce au soleil du tropique mouvant
    Les flots tièdes et bleus de la mer des Antilles" (21).
3. "soirées ouatées de brise marine fraîche et adorable, aux promenades silencieuses sur l'épais tapis de sable et . . . la soie de ses cheveux" (27).
4. "arpentée nuit et jour d'un sacré soleil vénérien" (34).
5. "une vieille misère pourrissant sous le soleil, silencieusement; un vieux silence crevant de pustules tièdes, l'affreuse inanité de notre raison d'être" (34).
6. "rêves avortés, le fleuve de vie désespérément torpide dans son lit, sans turgescence ni dépression, incertain de fluer, lamentablement vide, la lourde impartialité de l'ennui, répartissant l'ombre sur toutes choses égales, l'air stagnant sans une trouée d'oiseau d'air" (40).
7. "je crois que je me définirais comme étant un homme de terre, de montagne et de feu. Dans ma sensibilité la montagne joue un très grand rôle parce que je suis martiniquais, et parce qu'à l'horizon de la sensibilité martiniquaise il y a toujours la présence de la montagne" ("Le cri" 101).
8. "—les volcans éclateront, l'eau nue emportera les taches mûres du soleil et il ne restera plus qu'un bouillonnement tiède picoré d'oiseaux marins—la plage des songes et l'insensé réveil" (*Cahier* 34).
9. Dernièrement il y a eu une discussion avec Césaire. Il a dit, "tant qu'il y aura des nègres qui pensent, la négritude existera." Moi, je ne crois pas. Je crois justement qu'au fur et à mesure que les nègres réfléchissent, ils s'aperçoivent . . . que les nègres n'existent pas. Que c'est le racisme des blancs qui a fait de tous les hommes à peau noire, si vous voulez, des personnages identiques, et tu sais imaginer que tous les hommes à peau noir avaient la même culture, les mêmes attentes, peut être voir la même langue, etc. Au fur et à mesure on s'aperçoit que le monde noir est complètement divers. Il y a *des* peuples noirs avec des histoires différentes, particulières, des ambitions différentes, des problèmes différents. Et je crois au fur et à mesure on se rend compte qu'il ne peut pas avoir de négritude, c'est-à-dire, de communauté tout à fait flux qui s'appuit sur la couleur des indivus. Je crois que la négritude est condamnée . . . . Et que ce qui va paraître, ce sont des littératures régionales . . . qui vont prendre le dessus.
10. "une annihilation de la fausse universalité, du monolinguisme et de la pureté" (*Eloge* 14).
11. "l'identification est l'ennemie de l'identité" (193).
12. "Quoi? Quelle Afrique? . . . Y'a plus d'Afrique fout! Où c'est d'abord, l'Afrique? Où sont les sentiers, les traces de retour? Y'a des souvenirs du chemin sur les vagues" (213)?
13. "dialectique réamorcée entre nature et culture antillaises" (*Discours* 133).

14. "sont de type éthiopien, tranquilles comme la Soufrière, et les Martiniquais des Hamitiques, bouillonnants comme la montagne Pelée" (218).
15. "grossières simplifications jalouses."
16. "Nous, les Antillais, nous sommes les débris d'une synthèse" (226).
17. "Des racines sous-marines: c'est-à-dire dérivées, non implantées d'un seul mât dans un seul limon, mais prolongées dans tous les sens de notre univers par leur réseau de branches" (*Discours* 134).
18. "Pas de dénouement, surtout pas de fin: encore de la soif, avec le feu du coeur et du volcan, le vent des cyclones et des baisers, l'eau des sources et de la mer" (Maximin 281).

Works Cited

Arnold, A. James. *Modernism & Negritude*. Cambridge, Massachusetts: Harvard University Press, 1981.
Barnabé, Jean, Raphael Confiant, and Patrick Chamoiseau. *Eloge de la créolité*. Paris: Gallimard, 1986.
Baghio'o, Jean-Louis. "Bourrasque." *La Poésie Antillaise*. Ed. Maryse Condé. Nancy: Editions Fernand Nathan, 1977.
Césaire, Aimé. *The Collected Poetry*. Trans. Clayton Eshleman. Berkeley: University of California Press, 1983.
Chamoiseau, Patrick. *Chronique des sept misères*. Paris: Gallimard, 1986.
Condé, Maryse. Personal interview. 15 July, 1990.
Dash, J. Michael. "Le cri du Morne: La Poétique du paysage césairien et la littérature antillaise." *Soleil éclaté: Mélanges offerts à Aimé Césaire*. Ed. Jacqueline Leiner. Tubingen: Gunter Narr Verlag, 1984.
Glissant, Edouard. *Caribbean Discourse: Selected Essays*. Trans. J. Michael Dash. Charlottesville: University of Virginia Press, 1989.
Glissant, Edouard. *Le discours antillais*. Paris: Editions du Seuil, 1981.
Maximin, Daniel. *L'Isolé soleil*. Paris: Editions du Seuil, 1981.
Saint-Aurèle, Poirié de. "Les Antilles." *La Poésie Antillaise*. Ed. Maryse Condé. Nancy: Editions Fernand Nathan, 1977.
Thaly, Daniel. "L'Ile lointaine." *La Poésie Antillaise*. Ed. Maryse Condé. Nancy: Editions Fernand Nathan, 1977.
Thomarel, André. "Parfums et saveurs des Antilles." *La Poésie Antillaise*. Ed. Maryse Condé. Nancy: Editions Fernand Nathan, 1977.

# Afro-Cuban Culture, Ecology, and Climate in "La comparsa" by Felipe Pichardo Moya

Luis A. Jiménez

In his book on Afro-Cuban folklore, Fernando Ortiz dwells on the structures of activities present in songs and dances in Afro-Cuban lyrics. Using the dancing patterns of the *pareja* (couple) and the *multitud* (crowd), he finds in its rhythms a physical release of human tensions and socio-cultural inhibitions. For Ortiz, their frantic movements imply a muscular liberation that has some therapeutic properties for the community as a whole (183). A similar cultural and environmental or climatological connection[1] is depicted by G. R. Courthard in his study of literary "Afro-Cubanism." His analysis centers on the period 1920-40 and covers the most representative poets of the genre: José Z. Tallet, Ramón Guirao, Emilio Ballagas, Alejo Carpentier and Nicolás Guillén, the latter being the only non-white *negrista* exponent of the *Afrocriollo* movement.[2] The critic also suggests that Afro-Hispanic characters, male and female, react to music by expressing frenzied contortions. Furthermore, he refers to music, instruments, rum-drinking and voodoo rituals as ways in which dancers engage with intense bodily actions like "distorted arabesques" (31).

It may be said that a cultural approach to Afro-Cuban poetry cannot be complete unless it includes an interpretation of the physical processes that go on in the human body in response to environmental stimuli. Just as structures such as the lungs, the heart and the liver function in relation to physiological needs, so also do organized sociocultural institutions—music and dance—represented in the genre. In the following discussion I will show how Eugene P. Odum's principle of community ecology can be applied to "La comparsa" (costumed carnival groups) by Felipe Pichardo Moya (1892-1957), a poem that first appeared in the Havana magazine *Gráfico* in 1916.[3]

The custom itself is connected as much to climate as to culture, for it is only in tropical regions that *comparsas* of this sort are found.

For Odum the more purely biological factors of modern ecology are the relationship of organism to organism. These are real entities, living in any given territory, at a given time. Under certain climates, they are intimately linked together to what he calls a "biotic community" (145). In his opinion the study of group organizations should deal with the relationship of population to external aspects as well as to internal dynamics (487). Hence, in Odum's views, human society differs from all other living groups because of man's flexibility in behavior and his ability to control his own surroundings. This hypothesis associates man's essential physical and climatological environment to his cultural traditions. The interaction of both—environment and tradition—causes the formation of different ecosystems. Thus, one might refer literally to the severe Indian demographic conditions of the high, cold Andean region reflected in the *indigenista* novel or to the tropical cultural landscape of Afro-Cuban dancers in a carnival, poetically recreated in "La comparsa."[4]

Pichardo Moya was a lawyer and archeologist in his native Camagüey province. As a poet, he belongs to what many critics call "Cuban Post-Modernism." But it is perhaps for the early publication of this particular poem that he has been considered a forerunner of Afro-Cuban poetry (Ruiz del Vizo 18). We may note, however, that the use and abuse of dark-skinned people became a literary fashion in white aesthetics during and after the second decade of the twentieth century. Spanish American intellectuals, following the lead of the European negrophilia, sought inspiration in the culture of the African and his continent. This path was also used in the Antilles to bring all segments of the community into national life and art (Jackson 21). Courthard explains that the racial preoccupation in Afro-Antillean cultural history went hand in hand with the folkloric subsoil and its social ecology (174).

"La comparsa," with its highly suggestive title, shows a communal dance, one of the many cultural activities performed mainly by Black dancers during the annual carnival street celebrations in the Island of Cuba. It appears that the *comparsa* was created in the nineteenth century for the celebration of the feast of the Epiphany—the Three Kings Day. Historically, it succeeded the role of the *Cabildos*,[5] and during that period the *comparsa* had a genuine affiliation with this festivity, characterized by its large crowds of people.

In biological terms, biotic communities are often compared to composite organisms with their own laws and properties. Just like the *comparsa*, they clearly show distinctive cultural patterns related to their natural environment, climates and ecosystems (Odum 490). Elias Canetti has offered a useful classification of the term by distinguishing its various types of significant characteristics. One of them is the "rhythmic crowd" (30) which I will use for my study of "La comparsa."

Reflections of climate may be seen in the stanza that follows the opening refrain that begins with a maddened crowd singing and dancing in the silence of the tropical night. The speaker recreates a particular territory or micro-environment through a "solitary street," comparing the single line of the "comparsa" to "a colossal serpent." This zoomorphic imagery is closely related to the African climatic and ethnocultural traditions in which the serpent symbolizes a deity. Nevertheless, it is curious to note its close ties to Cuban reality, since between 1886 and 1914 there were six outstanding carnival groups in Havana alone: "The snake," "The beautiful bird," "The sparrow hawk," "The frog," "The scorpion" and "The small scorpion" (Urfe 184). Their zoomorphic names are an indication of the cultural continuity between Africa and Cuba.

Especially noteworthy in a *comparsa* is the collective spirit of the community manifested in what may be described as an emotional call-and-response pattern to music. This strophic modality is a common characteristic of both African and Afro-Cuban poetry. In fact, it constitutes the refrain (*estribillo*) which is repeated seven times in the text: "Por la calleja solitaria / se arrastra la comparsa como una culebra colosal" (Through the solitary street / crawls the costumed carnival like a colossal serpent). The festive crowd, like ponderable matter, gains momentum when children, women, and men sing and dance to the "impulso irresistible de los palitos y el timbal" (irresistible impulse of small percussion sticks and drums) a force that results in the striking socio-cultural interaction of the group as a whole.

It is easy to observe how climatic conditions, music, and dance produce their physiological effect on the "comparsa" dancers. As Canetti and Odum put it, the urge to grow in numbers is a supreme attribute of crowds and ecological communities (16, 487). The participants want to seize everyone within reach, thus establishing a physical bond to one another through the contact of their bodies. Their bonding is noticeable in the fact that every strong sensation, emotion or excitement felt has a tendency to cause muscles to tremble in unison: "los unos detrás de los otros en una fila inacabable, / van agarrados por los hombros con un temblor epilepsial" (some go behind others in an everlasting line / held by the shoulder with an epileptic tremor).

Closely related to climate is Ortiz's book on Afro-Cuban folkloric music that explores these expressions of emotions that originate with an auditory communication. He clearly states that feelings combine with muscular movements, and can be transmitted to the lungs, the heart, and the human nervous system by means of rhythm (180, 253). In "La comparsa," the countenance of the community becomes distorted into every shape permitted by the muscles of the face and body (Canetti 33). Grimaces are instantly portrayed by the dance performers in exact unison: "Los ojos brillan en las órbitas / chispeando como un puñal en la siniestra oscuridad, / y los cuerpos se descoyuntan con una furia demoníaca" (The eyes sparkle in their orbits / like a knife in the sinister darkness, / and their bodies are disjointed with a devilish madness). Such a Terpsichorean "devil-may-care" atmosphere represented a typical cultural performance in the climate of the Cuban carnival prior to 1961.

In a "rhythmic crowd" ecosystem everything depends on quick movements. Concretely, the physical stimuli function in gradual sequences. In the *comparsa*, the steps taken by their feet repeat and multiply in the same way that cells, tissues, and molecules do. The sound of their steps does not die away, for they are constantly increased in numerical proportion. Just as the cosmos itself can be understood as a vast harmonic system of ratios, the *comparsa* also becomes a relationship of mathematical dimensions. In the poem, musical tones and their corresponding steps are poetically translated in terms of numbers. Such numbers also hint at the Afro-Cuban cultural survival after so many years of slavery: "Uno, dos, tres, cuatro / con sus trajes más chispeantes y el paso *esclavo* del compás, / Dan pasos hacia el frente, / y luego dan otro hacia atrás / como en un rapto de locura" (Ruiz 20). (One, two, three, four / with their most sparkling costumes and the slave step of the beat, /they move forward, / then they move backwards / like a fit of madness). As long as the participants are dancing, they exert an attraction on their community. Moreover, their excitement grows progressively, reaching a climate of frenzy as long as they feel as one.

Every section of the dancers' bodies capable of movement gains a life of its own. As they manage to hold torches and gigantic lanterns in "a painful equilibrium," another kind of force "seems to throw them off." The rhythmic "everlasting line" of the "comparsa" mirrors a distinctive geometrical structure of activity (Ruiz 20). Acrobatic feats are executed in a series of short turns and angles in which all motor performances are coordinated as to resemble a choreographic routine. In fact, Afro-Cuban popular music has been viewed as "generatrix rhythmic cells" (Ortiz 272-273). The reader captures the euphoric climate in this poetic description: "Y, de pronto, a un vago impulso, / atravesando las aceras como en un rápido zig-zag, / hacen temblar a las farolas con un temblor epilepsial" (Ruiz 20). (And on a vague impulse, / crossing the sidewalk in a rapid zig-zag, / they make the lantern tremble with an epileptic shaking).

Epileptic "tremor" and "shaking," words used throughout the poem, are usually marked by the disturbed electrical rhythms of the central nervous system. Considered in these terms, it can be assumed that the emphasis on the internal dynamics of the bodies may be explained as the influence of wave excitations transmitted to the nerve fibers and muscles of the dancers. In this physiological context, anatomical parts appear superimposed on one another as women, transfixed by the singing of the "great tumult," swing their stretched arms extended and shaking their shoulders and hips. As long as their ears are listening to the expected melody, the whole body of the dancers will move to a common rhythm. The magic of the scene is harmonically recreated in the poem when "suben las voces por encanto, / y luego vuelven a bajar; / la música, ronca y monótona, va evocando mil raras cosas" (Ruiz 21). (voices rise through enchantment, / and then they are lowered / the music passes evoking a thousand rare things).

Despite wide cultural variety, all human societies have certain essential features in common. These involve the incorporation of individuals into crowds, musical communication through dancing, systems of kinship and myth, and rituals which are somehow related to the social group's past and its continuation into the present. Because of these common features, the conscious experience of the "rhythmic crowd" embraces the formation of behavioral patterns of interconnection. Memories also play a crucial role in the reconstruction of cultural traditions that cannot be always explained genetically. Instead, they depend on other kinds of transmissive processes which take place within the learning context of the group (Sheldrake 201, 237). In the case of Afro-Cuban culture, music and dance are best conveyed through the mystical transmission of past religious beliefs.

Since most African rituals are uttered by dancing to musical beats, it is no surprise to find all these components strongly operative in "La comparsa." Up to now, the crowd has shown an uncontrollable rhythmic urge to be part of the carnival. Pursuing the same line of thought a little further, one finds that in the last stanzas the poem sharply shifts to a more religious texture. This shift is accomplished through the recitation of the mysterious chants performed by an old man. These chants, in Ortiz's own terminology, belong to the so-called "fetishist sects" (128). Just to show the flavor of mystical symbiosis that surfaces in the new spectacle, I partially quote the verses in which the speaker presents his description of the event:

Entre dos filas de mujeres
que se contorsionan nerviosas como mordidas por Satán,
va un alto anciano tembloroso en cuyos ojos luce el fuego
de una mirada casi irreal.
Lleva su cetro entre las manos y murmura con voz opaca un
misterioso sortilegio que sólo él puede rezar,
como un rezo de ritual (Ruiz 21).
(Between two lines of women

with nervous contortions like those bitten by Satan,
appears an old man shaking whose eyes emit the fire
of an almost unreal sight.
He holds his scepter and murmurs in an opaque voice
a mysterious sorcery that only he can pray,
like a ritual prayer.)

Within the physical interaction of the two rows of women dancers, there is an "old shaking man," the only individualized character introduced in the text. He carries a scepter, a symbol of his native Africa. The flamelike expression in his eyes is indicative of a mystical experience that is just about to take place. The passage also brings into the scene the "mysterious sorcery" presented through the murmurs of the chant. The old man's monotonous and repetitive recitations help to create a mystical illusion of the supernatural, and will eventually lead to a possession rite in the poem. From a spiritual point of view, the *rezo del ritual* (ritual prayer) described by the speaker is one of the most outstanding manifestations of the *santería* (voodoo) cult. It must be added that historically the origins of some Afro-Cuban poetry elements are found in these religious chants as well as in the "Songs of the Cabildo."[6]

The influence of climate appears in the old Black man's utterings of his mysterious chants that evoke the memory of his remote African land. In terms of geography, the speaker underscores the importance of this spiritual invocation meant for the worship of an ancestral king-god: "la gloria del trono donde él reinara cuando niño" (Ruiz 21) (the glory of the throne where he ruled as a child). In the scientific context, his genetic mutation (man-child) is a clear example of atavism by which a living organism comes into resonance with "fields of an extinct type," reappearing again in the form of an archaic structure (Sheldrake 286). Additionally, the spiritual presence of the forefather stresses his role model as a guardian of cohesion and discipline within the biotic community.

However, through the chants, what an alert reader (or listener) really depicts is the speaker's persistent attempt to expose the anthropological ingredients of the old man's African heritage. By means of reconstructing an ecosystem, the mystical (and somewhat mythological) experience refers back to transcultural climatological and environmental elements: "allá en su selva ecuatorial, / entre las tribus de guerreros y de sagrados sacerdotes / que lo adoraban al pasar" (Ruiz 21; there in his equatorial forests, / among the warriors' tribes and sacred priests / that worshipped him upon passing.) The use of this socio-historical rite reflects the need to interconnect the land, the climate and the culture. As the "comparsa" comes to an end, one can see "los torsos de caoba," (the ebony chests) and under the extreme heat of the night "el sudor hace rebrillar" (sweat makes them glisten). The sense of community across the boundaries of time and space also links the continuity of several generations of the living and the dead. A linkage suggested by the final stanza, where an uninterrupted sequence of "sombras [que] tiemblan en las casas / con un temor al más allá: la música va evocando mil cosas raras" (21; [shadows] (that) shake in the houses / with a fear of life after death: music is evoking a thousand rare things.)

To sum up, the "rhythmic crowd" ecosystem in this poem vividly communicates the exchange of behavioral patterns within the socio-cultural and climatological realm that characterizes Afro-Cuban poetry. In the "comparsa" this communication was accomplished by corporal movements, by distinctive physiological reactions and in a variety of other ways, the most remarkable being the dancers' sudden incitement to music and dance. My application of the "community ecology" hypothesis to the text has been intended to illustrate how the collective feelings of the group are molded to a climatic and ecological unity and how in Afro-Cuban poetry the widely-shared customs of the Black community are expressed by systems of ceremonies rooted in the African tradition.

Notes

1. Cintio Vitier shares a similar socio-biological point of view. He sees in Afro-Cuban poetry a direct influence from the nineteenth-century Positivism of Herbert Spenser (1820-1903) and Charles Darwin (1809-1882) (308).

2. A different position is that of Richard L. Jackson who categorically questions Guillén's affiliation to the *negrista* mold of drums, rumba and voodoo used by Ortiz, Ballagas, Carpentier and other writers. In the critic's opinion Guillén rejected *negrismo* to propagate his own theory of *mulatez* (26-27).

3. See Hortensia Ruiz del Vizo. I am quoting from her anthology (20-21).

4. The geographer Hilgard O' Reilley Sternburg has pointed out that man's culture can only be understood in terms of traditions, beliefs, and taboos. Man is indeed the bearer of a congenital hereditary and cultural patrimony (281).

5. An article by Odilio Urfé deals briefly with the historical event. *Cabildos* were organizations of Freed Blacks, Creoles or Africans whose participation in collective recreational activities maintained social cohesion among the same ethnic group.

6. Urfé considers that for Cuban historiography these songs constitute an indispensable source to unravel the African roots of Cuban dance and music (171). See my article on Tallet's rumba.

Works Cited

Canetti, Elias. *Crowds and Power.* New York: Viking Press, 1962.
Courthard, G. R. *Race and Colour in Caribbean Literature.* Oxford: Oxford University Press, 1962.
Jackson, Richard L. *Black Literature and Humanism in Latin America.* Athens: University of Georgia Press, 1988.
Jiménez, Luis A. "Facts and Poetry: Afro-Cuban Folklore in José Z. Tallet's *La rumba.*" *Diaspora* 2 (1993): 26-40.
Odum, Eugene P. *Fundamentals of Ecology.* Philadelphia: W.B. Saunders, 1966.
O'Reilley Sternburg, Hilgard. "A Geographer's View of Race and Class in Latin America." *Race and Class in Latin America.* Ed. Magnus Morner, New York: Columbia University Press, 1970.
Ortiz, Fernando. *La africanía de la música folklórica de Cuba.* La Habana: Publicaciones del Ministerio de Educación, 1950.
Ruiz de Vizo, Hortensia. *Black Poetry of the Americas: Bilingual Anthology.* Miami: Ediciones Universal, 1972.
Sheldrake, Rupert. *The Present and the Past.* New York: Times Book, 1988.
Urfé, Odilio. "Music and Dance in Cuba." *Africa in Latin America.* New York: Holmes and Meiers Publishers, 1977.
Vitier, Cintío. *Lo cubano en la poesía.* La Habana: Departamento de Relaciones Culturales, 1958.

Notes on the Authors

CLEMENTINA R. ADAMS was born in Barranquilla, Colombia. She is currently an Assistant Professor of Spanish in the Department of Languages at Clemson University Language Department, Clemson University. She received her B.A. in Spanish and Literature from Atlantic University, Barranquilla, Colombia in 1969, and the M.S. from Florida State University in 1974, and the Ph.D. from Florida State University in 1984.

Her areas of research interest include contemporary Hispanic and Afro-Hispanic literature and culture. Rencent articles include "Extra-Sensorial Realism in *El Fabricante de Máscaras,* by Jaramillo Levi"; and "Women's Masks Through Life: Narrative Voices in *La noche de Ina* and *La juala del unicornio,*" by Hilda Perera; "Abriendo una Brecha en la Tradición del Poder Racial y la Aristocracia Social: Un Análisis de la Obra *El Regalo* de Rosario Ferré." Currently, she is completing a book on Afro-Hispanic Women Writers (an annotated anthology).

CIDA S. CHASE, a native of Costa Rica, is a Professor of Spanish at Oklahoma State University. Her fields of specialization are Twentieth Century Latin American Fiction and Foreign Language Methodology. She has numerous publications on these areas, including a book on the long fiction of Alejo Carpentier.

Professor Chase currently concentrates her research endeavors on modern Mexican fiction and feminine Hispanic narrative. She is responsible for the establishment of Chicano Literature and Civilization courses at her institution. Moreover, she is a territorial speaker on Latin American and Chicano Literature for the Oklahoma Foundation for the Humanities.

LEONARD A. CHEEVER is Professor of English at Stephen F. Austin State University where he has taught since 1967. His specialty is comparative literature and he has published over forty articles, mostly on American/Latin American literature and on authors such as Jorge Luis Borges, Julio Cortázar, John Updike, Juan José Arreola, Saul Bellow, Manuel Puig, Stanislaw Lem, Pablo Neruda, Carlos Fuentes, Gabriel García Márquez, Jorge Amado, and William Golding. He has served four times as a Fulbright Professor: in Argentina (1972); in Guatemala (1973-74); in Costa Rica (1988); and most recently at the University of Monterrey in México.

GARY S. ELBOW is Professor of Geography at Texas Tech University and Director of the Latin American Area Studies Program and the Center for Applied International Development Studies. He is a specialist in Latin American geography with research interests in Central America and the Andean Republics. He is a Contributing Editor for the *Handbook of Latin American Studies* and the author or co-author of several pre-collegiate and college-level textbooks. He has been a Fulbright scholar in Costa Rica and Ecuador. His primary reserarch interests include urbanization, agricultural change, and the relationships of geography and literature.

LUIS A. JIMÉNEZ received his Ph.D. in Latin American Literature from The Johns Hopkins University. He is currently the Chair of the Modern Language Department at Florida Southern College where he also teaches Afro-Hispanic culture and literature. Professor Jiménez is the author of *Literatura y sociedad en la narrativa de Manuel Gálvez* (1990), *El arte autobiográfico en Cuba en el siglo xix* (1995), and articles on Juan Francisco Manzano, Julián del Casal, Juan Rulfo, Octavio Paz and Julia de Burgos, among others.

JACK JORDAN received his Bachelor's Degree from Vanderbilt University, his Master's Degree from George Washington University and his doctorate from The University of Virginia. He is currently an Associate Professor at Mississippi State University. His most recent publication is *Marcel Proust's A la recherche du temps perdu: A Search for Certainty* (Summa Publications, 1993). The present interview with Maryse Condé and an interview with Patrick Chamoiseau were both made possible by a research grant from Mississippi State University. Professor Jordan is currently working on the relationship between identity and Creole language, as seen in the novels of Patrick Chamoiseau.

WENDELL E. MCCLENDON, to whom this volume is dedicated, focused his research on stylistics in the nineteenth-century French novel. He published articles on George Sand, Honoré de Balzac, and Emile Zola. At the time of his death in 1992, he was working on a book about the use of color imagery in Zola's novels. He was awarded tenure and promoted to Associate Professor posthumously by Texas Tech University, where he taught for 8 years.

GEORGE MCMURRAY is a native of Grinnell, Iowa and a graduate of the University of Nebraska. He has published reviews, articles and books on contemporary Spanish American literature. His books include *Gabriel García Márquez, José Donoso, Jorge Luis Borges,* and *Spanish American Writing Since 1941: A Critical Survey.* At present he teaches Spanish American literature at the University of Montana.

ROBERT J. MORRIS is presently a professor of Spanish in the Humanities Division of Lander University. He has also taught at the University of Cincinnati (1968-71) and Texas Tech University (1971-1991).

ROSEMARY NIELSEN and ROBERT H. SOLOMON teach at the University of Alberta in Edmonton, Canada, in the Classics and English Departments respectively, and for more than a decade they have written on Horace and Catullus and their English translators, from Aphra Behn and John Milton to A. E. Housman, Gerard Manley Hopkins, and Ezra Pound. Their work has appeared in *Ramus, Latomus, Revue Belge,* and *The Canadian Journal of Comparative Literature:* and it has led to interdisciplinary teaching, as well as to conference papers presented in Canada, the United States, Australia, and New Zealand.

STEPHEN T. NEWMYER is Professor of Classics at Duquesne University in Pittsburgh, Pennsylvania. He received his Ph.D. from the University of North Carolina in 1976. He is author of a monograph on the occasional poetry of Statius, of textbooks on Statius and Herodotus, and of twenty-five articles on classical literature, on the classical tradition in later literature and in the arts, and on ancient medical science, in particular on classical and Jewish climatological theory. At present he is at work on a book on Plutarch's views on animal-related issues and how his views have survived and have been developed in current literature on animal rights.

RAQUEL ROMEU earned the Ph.d. from the University of Havana and is Professor of Spanish language and literature and Chair of the Department of Foreign Languages at Le Moyne College in Syracuse, New York. She also teaches Spanish and Spanish American civilization courses. In addition to various articles, she has published two books: *Eugenio María de Hostos: antillanista y ensayista* and *La mujer y el esclavo en la Cuba de 1840*. Her main area of interest is the Caribbean. She has worked extensively on Lydia Cabrera and has written several papers on Mario Vargas Llosa.

STAFFORD LIBRARY
COLUMBIA COLLEGE
1001 ROGERS STREET
COLUMBIA, MO 65216